motörhead
IN THE STUDIO

motörhead
IN THE STUDIO

JAKE BROWN
WITH
LEMMY KILMISTER

JB

JOHN BLAKE

Published by John Blake Publishing Ltd,
3 Bramber Court, 2 Bramber Road,
London W14 9PB, England

www.johnblakepublishing.co.uk

First published in paperback in 2010

ISBN: 978 1 84454 978 8

British Library Cataloguing-in-Publication Data:

A catalogue record for this book is available from the British Library.

Design by www.envydesign.co.uk

Printed in Great Britain by CPI Bookmarque Ltd, Croydon, CR0 4TD

1 3 5 7 9 10 8 6 4 2

Papers used by John Blake Publishing are natural, recyclable
products made from wood grown in sustainable forests. The manufacturing
processes conform to the environmental regulations
of the country of origin.

This book is dedicated to a handful of my most loyal metalhead friends: Richard and Lisa Kendrick, Joe Viers, Harry Slash, Paul Watts, Helen Royster, Alex Schuchard, Joshua T Brown and Andrew McDermott.

Acknowledgements

Project thank-yous: first and foremost, THANK YOU to Lemmy Kilmister for agreeing to participate in the writing of this book, some great interviews, for coming up with the *brilliant* cover concept and for adding what I hope is another tribute to the genre you founded, whether called speed rock, or thrash metal, or speed metal, as Lars Ulrich said – and I thoroughly agree after writing this book – 'Without Motörhead, there'd be no Metallica.' Next, a thousand thank-yous to John Blake Publishing Ltd for acquiring the rights to this very special project – personally for me and I know for MH fans and specifically to my editor at JB, Lucian Randall, for shepherding this project from acquisition through publication, I know it was a bit of a rollercoaster. To Jasmin St Claire for first introducing me to

Lemmy via the interview for your own book. Thanks to Todd Singerman for helping to facilitate the green-lighting for this project; thanks to the *amazing* collection of producers and engineers who contributed exclusive commentary to this project, including Tony Platt, Trevor Hallesy, Will Reid, Thom Panunzio, John Burns, Howard Benson, Ryan Dorn, Mark Dearnley, Chuck Reed, Peter Solley, Bruce Bouillet, Cameron Webb and Arabella Rodriguez. A *very* special thanks to the *ultimate* Motörhead fansite, www.Motorhead.ru, for the awesome interview/article archive and for overall having the most devoted Motörhead fansite online, and to the band's official website www.iMotorhead.com and their awesome webmasters G Paul May and Mark Jakeway – Spotmen Studios Inc at www.spotmen.com and anyone and everyone else who was involved in making this amazing project happen!

Personal thank-yous: to my wonderful parents, James and Christina Brown, my brother Sgt Joshua 'Jerry' Brown (*ret!*), congrats on Triple Crown! The extended Brown and Thieme families; Alex and Jackson Schuchard; Andrew and Sarah McDermott; Chris Ellauri (ongking.com); Sean and Amy Fillinich; Richard, Lisa and Regan Kendrick; Paul and Helen; Adam 'The Skipper' Perri; Matt and Eileen Pietz, congrats on the little one; Tim Woolsey; Penelope Ellis; Reed Gibbons; Ed Seaman, Rachel, Dave, Larry, Burt Goldstein and everyone else at MVD/Big Daddy Music Distribution who keep Versailles Records' product out there in stores; Harry Slash; Tony and Yvonne Rose and

Acknowledgements

everyone else at my long-time US publisher Amber Books
for everything you've always done and continue to do to
support my career, most recently with the release of
Prince: in the Studio, Vol 1: 197 5–1995; Jack David, David,
Crissy, Simon and everyone at ECW Press who has
supported the advancement of my writing career with
your publication of *Heart: in the Studio (Authorised)*, *Rick
Rubin: in the Studio* and forthcoming *Tori Amos: in the Studio*;
Kurt and Cris Kirkwood for *Meat Puppets: in the Studio*
(2010!); and Jasmin St Claire-Rhea: can't wait for the
book to be out – it's been a blast!

Contents

Acknowledgements   viii

Introduction: The Godfathers of Speed   xiii
Metal... Motörhead

Chapter One: *Motörhead* – 1977   1

Chapter Two: *Overkill* – 1978   17

Chapter Three: *Bomber* – 1979   29

Chapter Four: *Ace of Spades* – 1980   39

Chapter Five: *No Sleep 'til Hammersmith/*   49
Iron Fist – 1981/1982

Chapter Six: *Another Perfect Day* – 1983   65

Chapter Seven: *Orgasmatron/Rock'n'Roll* –   85
1986/1987

Chapter Eight: *1916* – 1990/1991   99

Chapter Nine: *March ör Die* – 1992   109

Chapter Ten: *Bastards* – 1993   123

Chapter Eleven: *Sacrifice* – 1995   139

Chapter Twelve: *Overnight Sensation* – 1996   159

Chapter Thirteen: *Snake Bite Love/We Are Motörhead* – 1998–2000   169

Chapter Fourteen: *Hammered* – 2002   183

Chapter Fifteen: *Inferno* – 2004   206

Chapter Sixteen: *Kiss of Death* – 2006   223

Chapter Seventeen: *Motörizer* – 2008   231

Conclusion: 2010 and Beyond...   247

The Godfathers of Speed Metal... Motörhead

We all grow up with our rock'n'roll heroes and, if we're lucky, we get to grow old with them, take our children to their shows and pass on our record collections to the next generation. It's a special arena that few bands earn the fan base to play in: the Rolling Stones, Aerosmith, the Who, Mötley Crüe, Metallica and, after close to 35 years at the helm of their very own metal niche, Motörhead.

According to *Rolling Stone*, 'Motörhead are the fathers of speed metal, the band that punks and headbangers could agree on in the 1980s (Metallica, for one, would not exist without them).' Founded by living legend Lemmy Kilmister, the band's lead vocalist/bassist/songwriter, *Billboard* magazine further noted of the band's profound influence that 'Motörhead's overwhelmingly loud and fast style of heavy metal was one of the most groundbreaking styles the genre had to offer in the late 1970s... Motörhead wasn't punk rock... but they were the first metal band to harness that energy and, in the process, they created speed metal and thrash metal.'

In the last 30 years, Motörhead has kept pace with several generations of multi-platinum metal offspring, from the aforementioned Metallica, to Slayer, Testament, Megadeth, Anthrax and Pantera, leading a sub-genre from the British underground with such hit classic LPs as *Overkill*, *Bomber*, *No Sleep 'til Hammersmith, Orgasmatron* and the legendary *Ace of Spades* among many others. Proving they remain more relevant than ever in the metal millennium, in 2005 Motörhead won their very first Grammy for Best Metal Performance and this past autumn had one of the best-charting album debuts of their career with *Motörizer*. Still, at the root of the band's longevity is what *Billboard* further pointed out as the unique fact that 'unlike many of their contemporaries, Motörhead continued performing into the next century... never changing their raging sound'. This was echoed by *Rolling Stone* magazine's observation that the band's 'sound remains the same, dependably raw and uncompromising across the decades'. *All Music Guide* concurred, noting that 'they were still cranking out quality albums in the late 2000s'.

This book explores the band's 26 hit albums via exclusive interviews with principle band members, producers, etc.

on the making of such classics as *Ace of Spades*, *Iron Fist*, *Overkill*, *Bomber*, *Too Little Too Late*, *Tear Ya Down*, *White Line Fever*, *Orgasmatron*, *Overnight Sensation*, *Stay Clean*, *No Class*, *Damage Case*, *Over the Top* and *Snake Bite Love* among countless others. One hundred per cent authorised by the band and featuring first-hand, exclusive interviews with founder/lead vocalist/songwriter Lemmy Kilmister, this is a guided tour through the making of all the classics by this truly legendary band.

Chapter One

Motörhead: 1977

Lemmy (Ian Kilmister) – bass, vocals
'Fast' Eddie Clarke – guitar
Phil 'Philthy Animal' Taylor – drums
Producer – Speedy Keen
Engineer – John Burns
Recorded – Escape Studios, Kent
Released – September 1977

Out of the ashes of space-rock band Hawkwind, Motörhead was born in 1975, founded by rhythm guitarist turned bassist and former Jimi Hendrix roadie Ian 'Lemmy' Kilmister, who recalled that, in the course of designing his new band, 'I wanted to be the MC5 basically – singer, guitar, bass and drums. Of course, it never quite works out that way, know what I mean? With my first

1

band, there was a three-piece rock band inside the centre of Hawkwind but I ended up doing it with Motörhead.' As Lemmy further explained in his autobiography, in addition to MC5, who been the 'big hero band of most of the underground... [I wanted to] throw in elements of Little Richard and Hawkwind. And that's more or less how it turned out. We were a blues band, really. Although we played it at a thousand miles an hour, it was recognisable as blues – at least to us it was; probably it wasn't to anybody else.' Kilmister further quipped in an interview with *Ink* magazine that 'maybe it was the drugs. I dunno. We were all doing speed when we started, but then again, I was doing it in Hawkwind. I've just always been in a hurry for everything. I'm a very impatient man.'

Rounding out his new band's line-up, Kilmister explained, 'Phil Taylor became my drummer because he kept coming over to my house and falling asleep over so I had to hire him. I also got a ride off him in a car with no windshield down to Rockville Studios in Wales and Phil was exactly what we needed. First, we had Pink Fairies guitarist, Larry Wallis but Eddie played really well, knew all the Yardbirds songs and he liked ZZ Top, so he worked well for the band as well.' In explaining why he chose to put down the guitar and take up bass, Lemmy – whose unique guitar-playing style of bass was a first for any heavy rock/metal outfit at the time – explained, 'I was a guitar player for years before I started playing bass. I played guitar in Hawkwind. So if I'd started playing bass straightaway, I'd be doing just bass things but I can't do that because my head's too busy thinking of things. I've got to stretch out, so I have always played the bass more like a guitar.' Elaborating in an interview with the band's biggest online fansite on why he took a liking to the bass as an instrument, Kilmister reasoned, 'I liked the skinny neck, you know. And I liked the weird shape too. I mean, it had nothing to do with the sound of the thing because it sounds awful. But I decided to fix the pickups. So I thought to give it some thunderbird pickups on the original one and it sounded like a monster. And it's all one piece of wood that's connected right through the body. And I liked that too. It's sturdy. So you can throw it down, it bounces and it doesn't break.'

Guitarist 'Fast' Eddie Clarke, in an interview with journalist David L Wilson, recalled jumping at the decision to join Lemmy's new band. 'I didn't have anything on at the time and Lemmy had a bit of a reputation so it was a chance for me to be in a band that already had a foothold. You do think a little bit like that when you are doing fuck all, you know. So I took the gig without really considering the music side of it. I knew that it was sort of hard rock or heavy because they played me the album that was just done and wasn't released. I was going to be rhythm guitarist originally so at the time I just wasn't thinking like that. I thought, yeah, this would be great, just to be playing! When I did finally get there and we settled down into a three-piece, I mean, to play the way that we played was because of Lemmy's sound – that is what changed it all. He plays [through] a lead Marshall amp with all the treble up and all the bass down and he also plays a Rickenbacker bass so if you can imagine the sound that you would get from that, it is kind of like a rhythm guitar more than a bass. When I played with Motörhead everything that I knew went out the window. It is like a whole new set of rules and Phil found the same thing because you are kind of islands within the band in a kind of way.'

As Lemmy revealed in his autobiography, 'At first I was going to call the band Bastard, a name which pretty much summed up the way I felt. But the guy who was managing us at the time, Doug Smith, didn't think it was a good idea. "It's very unlikely we're gonna get onto *Top of the Pops* with a name like Bastard," he pointed out. I figured he was probably right so I decided to call the band Motörhead. It made sense: and it's also the American slang for speed freak, so all the pieces fitted. And it was a one-word name; I believe in one-word names for bands – they're easy to remember. So I took my psychedelic-coloured amps, painted them flat black and Motörhead got underway... Late in [1975], we went down to Rockfield Studios, which is located on a farm in Monmouth, South Wales, to make a record. Dave Edmunds was going to produce it...

'Unfortunately, Edmunds only recorded four tracks with us: "Lost Johnny", "Motörhead" (two of the songs I wrote in Hawkwind), "Leaving Here" and "City Kids". Then Dave got signed to Led Zeppelin's label, Swan Song and they took him away. That was too bad because I really liked working with him – he was just like one of us... After Dave, we wound up with Fritz Fryer as producer... [He] finished up our record but he wasn't the man that Edmund was.

'This new line-up of Motörhead had been working together for a few months when Tony Secunda got us a deal to make a single for Stiff Records. So some time during the summer of 1976, we did "White Line Fever" – a song that the three of us had written together... All through the rest of 1976 and early 1977, we played gigs here and there, a lot of one-offs. By this point, the morale of the band was getting pretty low; all our efforts were getting us nowhere. We were starving, living in squats and nothing was happening. I was well prepared to keep going but Phil and Eddie wanted to give it up. It wasn't their band and they didn't have the commitment I did. So, finally, in April, after much debate, we decided to do a goodbye show at the Marquee in London and call it a day. Around this time, I hooked up with Ted Carroll from Chiswick Records. Ted made us an offer: "If you want to make a single, I'll schedule you for two days at Escape Studios in Kent."'

Once the band had been scheduled for the Escape Studios recording session, Lemmy recalled feeling as though everything was on the line, as 'that was our survival record, the label was giving us two sides, so that was two days in the studio and so we took a gamble and instead of the singles, did eleven backing tracks and no vocals in that time, brought him down to listen to it and played him the eleven tracks and

5

saw him rocking in the back of the studio, so I knew we had him there. So he said, "OK, finish the album," so that became the first Motörhead album.' Once the band's gamble had paid off and they'd been given a green light to finish a full studio-length LP, Lemmy recalled, via his autobiography, that the band chose to work 'with producer [John] "Speedy" Keen, who had been in a band called Thunderclap Newman, which had a No 1 hit in England with the song "Something in the Air".'

Assisting producer Keen on the sessions for Motörhead's debut LP was Escape Studios owner/engineer John Burns, who recalled the studio was 'located on a farm in Kent, in a wooden barn, with an extension for the control room, which was probably four metres by four metres. The barn itself was about four metres wide and maybe ten metres long. I had a Helius 24-channel console, running into a 16-track studio. I had bought that machine from Steve Marriott from Humble Pie and Small Faces. I had ten Neumann 87s, two Neumann 67s, the best of everything – absolutely the best of everything. I had been producing a lot of records in London and suddenly came into a lot of money when I produced *Selling England by the Pound* and *Lamb Lies Down on Broadway* for Genesis, so I reinvested it in my own studio. In the desk, Helius made their own compressors, so there were four or five compressors built into the desk, Auri compressors – all the top-of-the-line studios had them. There was a reverb in the console and I didn't use it when I was recording, more when I was mixing. I also had Revoxes for delays, tape delays, graphic equalisers, DSs and all that sort of thing. I also had an old BBC stereo mastering two-track, which was valve and must have been built in 1950. It weighed a ton.'

Upon arriving at the studio to work on the album, Burns recalled, 'There was a house next to the studio where the band stayed for four or five days and when they first set up, I thought, Christ! because they were very, very loud. My first impression of Lemmy was that of a leather-clad biker — that's what he looked like and I thought, well, this will be interesting, we'll see. But later, after a day or so, I immediately grew to like him because he was an intelligent guy — took a lot of speed but was very intelligent. Lemmy was very clear on what he wanted to do and everyone listened to what he wanted to say, and we all just got on with it.'

Indeed, Kilmister confirmed that once the band had begun recording, producer 'Speedy just put us down as we sounded, you know. We'd been doing this quite a while so it was easy, we just laid the songs all out.'

In offering further detail on the vibe producer 'Speedy' Keen created in the studio while working with the band, engineer John Burns offered, 'I had known Speedy ahead of working on the Motörhead record. He was an original rocker from the 1960s and was nurtured by Pete Townshend, and was one of them really. Speedy was really giving them atmosphere — not telling them what to play — because he had so much experience working in studios. He made the guys in the band relax. The band definitely respected him and he was just like, "Come on, guys, let's get on with it." It wasn't sit down and have heavy discussions, it was rock'n'roll, heavy rock.'

Working at a recording pace as frenzied as the band's natural sound, Lemmy revealed, 'We all stayed up straight for forty-eight hours to make it.' Engineer John Burns adds that they indeed 'did the basic tracks in two days and then the overdubs for guitar leads and vocals in the next three. And working at that pace, you just become another member of the band really and just looked at yourself as part of the making of the album. They were long sessions because there were large amounts of substances around in those days – hence the producer's name, Speedy, and he liked his speed. I joined him at times in that and we just got on with it.'

Confirming the latter, guitarist 'Fast' Eddie Clarke, in an interview with journalist David L Wilson, conceded that 'the drugs might have had something to do with that, I am not sure! I don't want to get too philosophical here. I must remember what state I was in at the time, we all were!' Continuing, engineer John Burns recalled, 'We did everything fast in the studio. I always liked to work really fast in those days and not hang around spending three hours getting a drum sound, so we'd get the drums done in half an hour and get on with it and were recording very quickly. I remember one night we stayed up all night recording "Train Kept A-Rollin'". All three of them were great rock stars –

Animal Phil was a real star on the drums and Fast Eddie was a star on the guitar, and they all gelled.'

Addressing the band's habit of mixing business and pleasure in the studio in their early days, guitarist 'Fast' Eddie Clarke, in an interview with his webmaster, would explain years later that, reflecting back, 'obviously, drink and speed were important in shaping the band... I was a dopehead. Speed was something that they all did and I soon found myself doing it as well. Then I realised that having a drink with the speed mellowed you out. That was how my drinking career got underway.'

Describing his set-up in the studio during tracking, Burns explained that 'the band always tracked live off the floor – bass, drums and guitar live. Sometimes we'd do a guitar again and the solos from Fast Eddie were done afterwards, as well as Lemmy's lead vocal tracks, but the rhythm tracks went down together. I always liked to work that way. I hate the way of recording where you put down the drums, then the bass, the guitar. Thankfully, Motörhead did too at that time. In terms of sound separation, there were no booths but we had screens made out of mattresses or sound-proofing stuff to absorb each instrument's sound and I would place a couple around the drums, a couple around the guitar amp, couple around the bass amps. They were using four stacks, you know, so you couldn't worry about separation too much. Obviously, you wanted a little bit of separation so if you made a little mistake you could repair it.'

As he went about tracking the band, the engineer would 'do sort of a run-through to check the sound but a lot of the things on that album were first takes. Our recording approach definitely wasn't, "Aw, we'll have to do that again guys, we messed up." It wasn't anything like that. They might come in, listen to the take and Lemmy would go, "Let's do another one," then they would go back out: *bang*, *bang*, *bang* and do another version. So if it wasn't first takes, it was second or possibly third takes. Usually, the first take would have been fine but Lemmy or Eddie might say, "We can do it better," or Phil would say that, so it was always that the second or third takes were better but not because the first take was crap. It was just stuff like, "We can put some more energy into it," stuff like that. So it would be beginning of the track to end of the track, come and listen, and keep it or do another.'

Turning to discussion of the band's specific members as they recorded, engineer John Burns explained, 'Animal Phil was a great drummer, mad as a hatter, brilliant though. In miking his drums, there would have been two Neumann 87 overhead mics, an AKG-224 E on the snare and, above the hi-hat, an AKG-451. I would have used both 87s and AKG-D20s on the toms and a D-25 on the bass drum. In miking Fast Eddie's guitar rig, I would have used an 87 and possibly a 67, which is the valve version of the 87 – they were both brilliant mics. Because they were a three-piece, I recorded the guitar in sort of a stereo, two-mic set-up. The monitors I had were fifteen-inch Hanoi rigs in

Rockwood cabinets, which places like Olympic Studios had, and then I used a Crown 700 pound power amp I had to drive the speakers. I also had two hanging speakers and two floor speakers, and I remember Speedy wanted to have the floor speakers really close to the desk and very loud. Fast Eddie was an excellent guitarist back then and blended in really well to form that band.'

Clarke added, in an interview with journalist David L Wilson, that, in playing with Lemmy in the studio, 'if you have got a big fat bass there you can kind of lose your guitar a bit. It takes the edge off of it and makes it sort of nice and warm but when you are playing with Lemmy and the drummer it just sort of makes it really hard and cutting so you can't really relax with the Motörhead sound. You are for ever having to keep your eye on it and hold it down as it were.'

Lemmy's bass sound was – and would continue to be – the most distinctive element of the band's recordings. 'He didn't play one string at a time, he was hammering it,' explains Burns, 'so his bass sound was their signature, his bass playing and his amp. The bass was recorded with an 87 and a Neumann 54 – it was a great mic.'

Once basic tracking had been completed, says Lemmy, the band 'took an extra three or four days to do the vocals'. In the course of tracking his vocals, the engineer explains that his chief focus was on 'pulling out everything I could do to help him do what he could do. Lemmy as a whole was a great character and his songs were him, so I didn't break anything down and say, "This is a better song than that one." I was recording Lemmy and his songs were written autobiographically. For vocals, I'm sure I used a 67 for Lemmy,' who further recalled that 'on the first record, there's only the one vocal, but that's evolved a lot since.'

Once the band had completed principle tracking and vocals, John Burns recollected feeling that, although 'the energy was fantastic on that album, the songs could have been better but that was Motörhead then. They were very, very loud and not a clean-sounding band, so it had to be recorded quickly because they just wanted to get it on and get it out, so the energy was enormously high – and obviously some of that was fuelled by substances – but I remember it was a great time and, after that, I needed a week to recover. I needed a week to recover from recording before we went in to mix.'

The clan regrouped for the album's mixing sessions at Escape. 'Basically, we did the whole recording there and would have had the entire album finished in about five days,' says Burns, 'but there was a technical problem when Speedy was mixing – where he was riding the channel faders right to the top, full up and then having the master gain right down, so it would go on to tape. So all the fader volumes were moved all to the very, very top, which caused some distortion and crackling sounds because he was basically overloading the desk. I think I gave them some more free time to make up for that crackling sound.'

To remedy the problem, the engineer decided to 'let

them come out with what they wanted and, in the end, Speedy gave me an executive-producer credit on the record because I did the majority of the mixing. After Speedy had overloaded the desk at my studio, I said, "I'll take the reins for the mixing because it's stupid to waste more money." So we decided to go to Olympic Studios to mix after we'd done the entire album at my studio, except for one guitar overdub Fast Eddie did. I remember we were all really tired by the time we got to Olympic and, thankfully, we were mixing on a Helius desk, which I liked because they were very functional and easy to run. It was very important because, in those days, the console was like an instrument. There was no automation. So you had to mix everything by hand, there was no memory. If you mixed one day and you listened the next day and didn't like something, you'd have to start over from scratch completely. You needed a desk that you could work really fast with and that, when you sat down, you could see the controls all right in front of you so you didn't have to stand up and look down while you were mixing. It was a bit like being in an airplane, I suppose, because the controls and EQs – which were also quite good – were facing you as you sat and mixed. With the mixing of the record, I was aiming to have first captured the band's live energy and volume on tape as best as possible and then, in mixing, just trying to get some form of separation on it with EQ, miking and stuff like that so you could control it a little bit.'

Once Burns and company had finished what Lemmy

remembered ended up being 'nineteen mixes of the album, they said, "Pick one you like," and I randomly said, "That one," and that's what came out'. Kilmister would further recall in his autobiography that the band 'recorded a total of thirteen songs for Chiswick and eight of them wound up on the album. Much of *Motörhead* was material from *On Parole*, which we re-recorded: "Motörhead", "Vibrator", "Lost Johnny", "Iron Horse", "Born to Lose" and "The Watcher". We also did two new songs: "White Line Fever" and "Keep Us on the Road", and a John Burnett song, "Train Kept A-Rollin'". The other songs that didn't wind up on the album included "City Kids", which was a B-side for the "Motörhead" single; a ZZ Top song called "Beer Drinkers and Hell Raisers"; "I'm Your Witchdoctor", a great song by John Mayall and Eric Clapton; "On Parole"; and an instrumental jam, which was appropriately called "Instro".

'Finally, Doug Smith took us back and got a deal with Bronze Records who had bands like Uriah Heep and the Bonzo Dog Doodah Band on its roster. It was just a single – they wanted to see how it did before they invested any more money in us – but it turned out to be the beginning of our long-awaited upward ascent. That summer we went into Wessex Studios in London and recorded "Louie Louie" with one of our own numbers, "Tear Ya Down", as a B-side. Covering "Louie Louie" was an idea Phil had come up with some months back when we were still with Tony Secunda. We'd been sifting through some old songs and I wanted to cover a Chuck Berry song, "Bye Bye Johnny", or something like that, but "Louie Louie" was a better choice really. I think we did a very good version of it – people tell me that it's one of the few times it's been recorded where the lyrics can be understood! Actually, I only got the first two verses and then the last verse was largely improvised. We produced it jointly with this guy Neil Richmond. We never did work with him again but he was good. Except for the weird clavioline thing he put in. The single was released on 25 August... By the end of September, it had gone up to No. 68 in the charts.'

Based on the success of the latter single, the band's full-length debut LP was released in November 1977, reaching UK No. 43. 'They were an exciting new band on their first album,' remembers John Burns. 'When the record came out in the papers, the reviews gave it five stars but said it sounded like the album was recorded on a cassette machine on the water. The band was so incredibly, incredibly loud and I think on the second album the sound was better, but on the first album Speedy and myself just let them get on with it. This was their sound and we let them do what they wanted to do, rather than trying to turn them into a polished, studio-sounding band because Motörhead was Motörhead. I always joke that I've worked with everybody from Genesis to Motörhead.'

Billboard magazine later acknowledged the arrival of Motörhead's unique brand of speed rock. 'Rock'n'roll had never heard the like... Though only a minor chart success, *Motörhead* patented the group's style: Lemmy's rasping vocal over a speeding juggernaut of guitar, bass and drums. Before this, hard rock was about musicianship and exhibitionism. Motörhead, conversely, returned mainstream rock to its most brutal base elements.' Lemmy, in selecting his own highlights from the band's debut LP, explained, 'I really like our version of "Train Kept A-Rollin'" and "Keep Us on the Road", I like that one too.' British rock and metal fans did as well and, following the band's signing to Bronze Records and an appearance on the legendary, star-making BBC music television show *Top of the Pops* on 25 October 1978, performing their cover of 'Louie, Louie', the band was green-lighted to re-enter the studio to record what would become their breakout second LP, *Overkill*.

Chapter Two

Overkill: 1978

Lemmy – bass, vocals, second guitar solo on 'Limb from Limb'
'Fast' Eddie Clarke – guitar
Phil 'Philthy Animal' Taylor – drums
Producer – Jimmy Miller – except 'Tear Ya Down'; **Producer** – Neil Richmond, remixed at Roundhouse Studios by Jimmy Miller
Engineers – Ashley Howe and Trevor Hallesy
Released – 24 March 1979
Peak Chart Position: UK No. 24

Perhaps some of Britain's tamer rock critics would call Motörhead's approach to rock'n'roll 'overkill' but, for the band, who would make their bones with the LP of the same name, heading into its recording, Lemmy was 'quite happy with the way things were going'.

With a rising profile as one of the country's most exciting

new rock acts, Motörhead attracted the attention of legendary record producer Jimmy Miller, who had overseen hit albums for the Rolling Stones and Traffic among others. In choosing Miller, the band had 'gone in the studio and done a track with him and it sounded good, so we went on and did the album', says Lemmy. 'We always do that, we do a sample track with a new producer and, if it sounds good, he gets to do the album. That's been a mainstay more or less over the years in how we work in the studio.' The frontman further recalled in his autobiography that, upon entering the studio with Miller, 'we only had a fortnight to record... Considering our chequered recording history, however, it was a world of time for us and, besides, being quick in the studio has always been natural. The whole experience was pure joy. We recorded at the Roundhouse Studios, which were next to the club of the same name in North London. Jimmy Miller was excellent, as was [engineer] Trevor Hallesy.'

The album was recorded between December 1978 and January 1979. 'Roundhouse Studios was the standard session studio,' says Hallsey, 'owned by Bronze records and originally designed for their own artists like Uriah Heep and mainstream pop artists like those who were signed to the label – this also included a lot of session musicians and string sections and that sort of thing. But eventually they allowed the studio to be used by external artists. The console at the studio was a board purpose-built for the studio by Clive Green, who had a company called Cadac.

Those boards were quite popular in the late 1970s and early 1980s. It was a massive L-shaped thing that had twenty-four outputs and thirty inputs, and had loads of switches and lots of relays, which were always sticking. So you'd route something to a channel and think it was going there but it actually wasn't, and you'd sort of have to rattle the relay out of it before it would flick in.

'Roundhouse was in high demand. The first purpose-built 24-track studio in London, it was opened in 1974 and, up until that time, studios had just been 16-track. Roundhouse had the first purpose-built 24-track studio and 24-track Studor tape machine. Some people, ironically, thought it was a downgrade going to 24 tracks because we were still using two-inch tape and so you're putting twenty-four tracks on a tape as opposed to sixteen. Each track was getting less tape width. Sixteen track sounds better because the quality is better and signal-to-sound is better but people wanted the tracks and were prepared to sacrifice a small amount of quality for the quantity of tracks – because ultimately they were more important.

'Obviously when you just had sixteen tracks to work with, you had to compromise on things more, where you'd record only so many separate tracks of drums and then do an overhead mix-down with the toms all mixed together, then a bass drum and snare drum track, and that was it – four tracks. Whereas with the 24-track, you could afford to spread out a bit and I think, in fact, on Motörhead's *Overkill* LP, I had ten tracks for drums. Of course, they had double

19

bass drums, so there were two bass-drum tracks and a snare track, a hi-hat track and I did the toms mix in stereo, so there were a couple of overhead mics and a separate ride-symbol mic, which is something we used to do. I also used to put a guitar pickup on the bottom of the snare, which I used to trigger the gate so that you could actually isolate the snare more in the balance and get any spillage from other drums on the snare track itself. So you would never use that signal on the actual outputs but as a trigger signal it was perfect because it kept everything in the background and picked up everything else around it. So it was a great trigger for a gate, and I'd normally put that on a separate track and then deal with the gate when we got to mixing.'

Expanding in greater detail on his approach to the mics used for speed drummer Phil Taylor, Hallesy recalls, 'We used AKG D-12s on the bass drums, which is pretty standard, one for the left and one for the right bass pedals on separate tracks, which would be quite close-miked inside the kick-drum, quite close to the skin. Then we had an SM-57 on the snare and for some songs an AKG-451 with the 20 DB pad (which went in the head of the mic to stop it from distorting).

'On the overheads I would use Neumann 87s and 47s and the tom mics were Sennheiser 441s. As a drummer, Phil had some stamina. For instance, when we recorded *Overkill*, it was a six-minute track and we did three or four takes of it, one after the other, and it's a very energetic track to play and he managed to keep up with that without flagging. I think we used one of the later takes as the master.'

To deal with the delicate business of capturing the band's ferociously loud live sound in the studio, engineer Trevor Hallesy tracked the band live. 'We had to separate everything off so we had reasonable separation on the drums and then, if we wanted to replace things afterward, we could. I think we might have kept some of the guitars and added more to them and we overdubbed the bass afterwards as well. Roundhouse, being designed in the 1970s, was a very dead studio – there was no live air in there at all – and we ended up taking out a lot of the carpets and putting new flooring down to give it a bit of liveness but that was *after* Motörhead recorded there. So at the time the band recorded *Overkill*, the live room was very dead – separation was fantastic in there. It wasn't an enormous studio but if you put a few screens around the guitar amps, that would be enough to separate it off from the drums and you could hardly hear it on the drum mics at all. So it was very good in that respect and seemed to work.'

Lemmy: 'In those days, we didn't have a pre-production process really, we just made sure we could all play the song at the same time. Back then, we all played all together in the studio at the same time and tried to get it right because that's how they did it then. Nowadays, you lay the drums first and then build on top of that. I like how we did it then because it saved a lot of fucking time.'

Engineer Trevor Hallesy: 'Motörhead was very professional; they'd been through it before and knew what was required. The band was well rehearsed and had been playing these songs for ages so when they came in the studio, it was pretty straightforward, to be honest. It was pretty quick and simple; they all knew what parts they had to play. Jimmy Miller might have suggested a few overdubs here and there but they generally got it sorted out between themselves, what they wanted, before we got started tracking.'

The band might have been together but producer Lemmy reveals that Jimmy Miller 'was messed up on smack for a long time, and he cleaned up for the first record and did really, really good'. Agreeing with Lemmy's characterisation of Miller's studio demeanour during the recording of *Overkill*, engineer Trevor Hallesy adds, 'On *Overkill*, Jimmy was there most of the time. He was very good at getting a good vibe in the studio, getting a good take out of a band, actually making them all comfortable. He was a lovely guy and was a good psychologist with the band. I don't remember him losing his temper ever in all the time I worked with him. He was good at keeping the status quo, that was one of his fortes. He was also very musical and a player himself.'

Once the band were recording, Lemmy recalled in his autobiography, 'As is usual with Motörhead, there were quite a few new songs that we'd already performed live. "Damage Case", "No Class", "I Won't Pay Your Price" and

"Tear Ya Down" were among those. Others we wrote in the studio. "Capricorn" was written in one night. Eddie's solo for that one, I recall, happened while he was tuning up. The tape was running while he was fooling around with his guitar and Jimmy added some echo. When Eddie finished tuning he came in and said, "I'll do it now," and Jimmy told him, "Oh, we got it." That saved us some money! "Metropolis" was another fast one. I went to see *Metropolis*, the movie... then I came home and wrote the song in five minutes. The words don't make any sense though. They're complete gibberish... But some of my lyrics have more meat on them."

When his attentions turned to recording his signature bass sound, Lemmy explained, 'My bass set-up has always been the same: 415s, 412s and two Marshall stacks. In the studio, I use one of the 412s and one of my hundred-watt amps and I like to play Rickenbackers. I like the shape of the neck and they have good pickups on them.'

Engineer Trevor Hallesy recalled a truly unique set-up in the studio for recording Lemmy wherein 'he had a Marshall cabinet he was using as his bass amp, a 4 x 12 guitar cabinet, and I remember looking at one of the speakers and finding it was pretty torn and, in actual fact, that's the speaker we ended up recording because it sounded the best for the sound Lemmy went for. It's like a distorted bass guitar sound really, he had. We used a Neumann 84 on it with a -10 DB pad in. We listened to each cabinet speaker to decide which was the best one and obviously this wasn't the best one, technically, but it was for this particular job and the fact that it was damaged seemed to help the sound we were looking for. My bottom-end challenge came more from the bass drums than the bass really because Lemmy's playing is more of a guitar-playing style than a bass-playing style – you have to use the drums for bottom end. So if you listen to Motörhead, the bass drums are really pounding away there and the bass is almost another guitar part.'

Hallesey tracked 'Fast' Eddie Clarke's guitar parts. 'When I was miking up Eddie Clarke's guitar amp, I tended to use a dynamic Shure SM-57 standard workhorse mic close to the speaker and a Neumann 87 further away, and I tended to blend the sound between the two, to sort of get the phase cancellation going on until you got the sound you wanted.'

The focus turned to recording Lemmy's lead vocal tracks. As fast as he played his bass, recalls the engineer, in the vocal booth he was also pretty quick. 'There were probably a few drop-ins here or there but nothing out of the ordinary. [It] wasn't a word-by-word job, or anything like that. It would have been a few takes and then stitch a few things in here or there. Lemmy sang singing up with the mic mounted on a live stand; it was a Neumann 87 and he would look up towards it while singing. He did all the harmonies on the *Overkill* album. I don't believe Eddie did any back-up singing on that record.'

Though everyone worked to make the tight recording schedule run smoothly, Hallesy remembers the touchiest player being Eddie Clarke. 'If there were any problems, it was normally with him and I don't know if he was being a bit of a perfectionist. Eddie was a little temperamental during overdubbing. It wasn't his fault really... by that point in the recording of the album, there's the rest of the band and the road crew and girlfriends and various things in the control room, and somebody's concentrating on trying to do a guitar solo, and you push the talkback button to talk to them and suddenly all they hear is a party going on in the control room. I remember he really did lose it one time and stormed out in a huff because somebody had said something about his guitar playing and, unfortunately, the talkback button was pressed down at the time and he heard it and... lost his cool, shall we say.'

Still, all in all, the engineer felt that things were going the right way, attributing that confidence in part to producer Jimmy Miller being 'a very good mixer. He did lots on the mixing of that album. *Overkill* had the same energy as his past projects. These were the days before automated mixing, so it was all hands on deck – the band and everyone would be involved. So I'd get a general balance up, and Jimmy would fool around with the faders and EQ until we'd fixed what the mix was. Then he would work out all the different knobs for the band members, so that everyone in the band would have an individual fader to move something at one point. It was standard in those days, before we had automated mixing, so the actual mix was more of a performance.

'You might have to do ten mixes, all exactly the same, but

then when you listen back they're not all exactly the same – there's subtle differences between them and perhaps one particular mix would have a better vibe than another, although basically it was the same balance. So that was quite a job, picking which mix, and sometimes we edited between mixes as well, where you'd have one mix with a better first chorus and another with a better second chorus, and you'd physically have to edit them in together – that's how we used to do it. That definitely went on during *Overkill* because, without automated mixing, the faders didn't move by themselves, so once you got a mix, that was it.

'If you did something wrong, you had to go back and do the whole mix over again and fix that piece or edit it in. Jimmy tended to prefer to just do another mix straight off and I think that was because he was into that feel of the mixing where he would really get into moving things around on the mix, and suddenly he'd push something up which we hadn't planned to do – just because he felt like it – and it was great, something spontaneous that would make the mix more exciting.'

Elaborating on the technical tools he and Miller utilised in the course of mixing the LP, engineer Hallesy recalls, 'Roundhouse had a reverb chamber we used on Motörhead while mixing, and the history of that was that Roundhouse was a big concert hall and theatre. In the basement they had a whole load of caves with tunnels into rooms, from back when it was a train engine-turning plant at the turn of the twentieth century. The studio had an area downstairs, which we completely tiled and put some speakers in and some microphones, and then we could send to it from the mixing console and use that room as sort of a natural-sounding live room. During the mixing of that album, we also added synthetic reverb and delays to give it a bit of space afterward. That's the way we did it in those days dealing with a dead room.

'I remember, for instance, putting stereo delays on the guitars, so you'd have the signal on one side and a slightly smaller delay on the other side. Also, on the drums, I added a little bit of small-room reverb. In those days, we didn't have quite as many digital reverbs, so I used just an echo plate with a delay on it, or a small delay with a bit of echo. We also had three or four EMT stereo plates in there, which we used for reverb during the mixing of *Overkill*. We might have used a shorter plate for guitar and then a delay plate for one of Lemmy's vocals, and a medium plate for Phil's drums but there's really not that much reverb on those early Motörhead albums, they're fairly dry, but definitely you'll find a little bit here or there just to sort of extenuate things.'

Lemmy picks out favourites from the album. '"No Class" – that one speaks for itself – and "Metropolis" and "Damage Case" I like a lot too.' He cited the inspiration behind 'Capricorn' in an interview with www.roughedge.com as being 'all about my star sign. Egotistical bastard!'

For Jimmy Miller, recalled Lemmy in his autobiography, *Overkill* 'was supposed to be something of a comeback album... which is exactly what it turned out to be. He had gotten very heavily into heroin... and he had lost it for a couple of years. Since *Overkill* charted right away — it eventually peaked at 24 — he got a lot of work from it.'

Released on 29 March 1979, *Overkill* took the British charts by storm, driven by the success of the singles 'Overkill' and 'No Class', and further working to establish a new brand of speed rock that inspired the *Daily Mirror* to proclaim, 'Their music is so loud it's like your brains being forced down your nose.' As the band's profile continued to rise along with the volume of their amplifiers, guitarist 'Fast' Eddie Clarke, in an interview with his webmaster, would years later explain that, at the time, the band was both unstoppable and indomitable because 'we had a bond and it went beyond whether you liked someone or not... I can't imagine being any closer to anyone else than those two... We felt almost indestructible because we'd had so much shit thrown at us and we'd decided that, no matter what happened, we were gonna fuckin' carry on.'

Chapter Three

Bomber: 1979

Lemmy – vocals, bass, eight-string bass
'Fast' Eddie Clarke – guitar, vocals on 'Step Down'
Phil 'Philthy Animal' Taylor – drums
Producer – Jimmy Miller
Engineer – Trevor Hallesy
Released – 27 October 1979
Peak Chart Position: UK No. 12

In response to the success of *Overkill* Motörhead re-entered the studio in July 1979, again with producer Jimmy Miller and engineer Trevor Hallesy, to track their third studio album, aptly titled *Bomber* – perhaps in celebration of the band's continued upward momentum.

Lemmy recalled, 'The label was pressuring us; we had *Overkill* up the charts so we went in and did *Bomber*, and it went higher than that.' In an interview with www.roughedge.com, Lemmy explained that the album's title track was 'inspired by the Len Deighton book of the same name. I suggest you read it – a monster of a book!'

Trevor Hallesy: '*Bomber* we did at Olympic Studios, which was a much bigger, liver room and it was the first time I had been outside Roundhouse Studios, which had been where I learned my craft. Olympic was a classic studio and had been going for years and had loads of hits out of it with the Stones, etc., and was really Jimmy's home studio where he made all his records out of.'

Sadly, by this time Miller himself was 'back on the shit [smack]', reveals Lemmy. 'Jimmy wasn't there as much, so we relied a lot more on the engineer on that album. The thing about Jimmy on *Bomber* was he had all these great stories about why he'd been gone for three hours scoring. I liked Jimmy a lot, it's a shame, he was great fun. In spite of all that, Jimmy was still a good producer, he still knew a good track when he heard it and did a good job on both the records but did a lot better on *Overkill* than *Bomber*.' In his autobiography, Lemmy added that Jimmy Miller 'was completely out of it and that got to be a little much. He would say he was going to the toilet for a moment, then he'd be in there for an hour and when he came out he'd be nodding. Once he went to the men's room and he never came back at all, so we went in and he was gone! Apparently, he'd left to find his dealer and we found him in his car, asleep at the wheel. Even when he was around, he was in absentia.

When we had the rough mix down we transferred it to quarter-inch tape and we started playing it back. Jimmy was nodding out in his chair the whole time we were setting it up and when the music came on, he woke with a start. He looked at us and started moving the faders up and down like he was working! And the tape wasn't even going through the desk – it was a bit of a giveaway.'

Engineer Trevor Hallesy was also very much aware of Miller's absence. 'He was in his home town then, so he had more chances to disappear. He would go out for a pack of cigarettes and wouldn't come back till the following day, so we just got on with it really. And then when Jimmy would get back, he would listen and normally say, "That's fine, that's fine."'

Yet, in spite of his deeper involvement in the production side of the album's recording, Hallesy still feels credit is due to the band for the way they got down to work without the guidance they might have expected under normal circumstances. 'I think it was more Lemmy who stayed in the captain's chair when Jimmy was gone. I was a relatively new engineer and didn't feel myself competent enough to take over Jimmy's position really. Lemmy'd been in a load of bands before Motörhead, so he was no spring chicken when it came to recording; he'd done it a bunch of times before, so he knew what he was doing. I'm sure if they'd wanted to they could have recorded that second album without Jimmy but he added a certain kudos to the scene, I suppose.'

It was largely left to the band and their engineer to get to grips with the technical set-up. 'It was a different experience working at Olympic from working at Roundhouse,' recalls Hallesy. 'First, because *Bomber* I recorded completely from scratch to mix outside of that studio and the console was a Helios, which was designed by the first maintenance engineer at Olympic – Dick Swettenham – and was purpose built and was a gigantic thing. A very odd board with these dial-type knobs, as opposed to faders, for monitoring. I remember thinking it looked like something out of *Star Trek* but it sounded great. It did have a very warm sound but was nothing compared to the Cadac console we had at the Roundhouse, which was a state-of-the-art, brand-spanking-new board. The Helios was just a bit confusing to use but, once I got the hang of it, it was OK. The studio had three Evan tape machines, which used this weird ISO-loop system, where the tapes would go in big loops around the heads – they were 24-track machines.'

Again tracking the band live off the floor for the album's basic tracks, as he had with *Overkill*, Hallesy quipped, 'When you're tracking Motörhead, it's not exactly complicated recording really. With *Bomber*, we were pretty much heading in the same sonic direction as the last album because everybody had been pretty happy with *Overkill*. So I was basically going for a similar sound. The studio provided the main difference in the sound. The recording process was fairly straightforward. I don't seem to remember any problems with it. Each member of the band knew exactly what they wanted to do and they all had agreed on this before they got in the studio, so it wasn't paint-by-numbers but it was pretty straightforward and we were just going through the process of getting it on tape.

'The separation in the live room was pretty good at Olympic. They had all sorts of booths. I mean, it was a *much* bigger studio – it's enormous. It's a massive, massive live room. They had orchestras and whatnot in there so it was very big, and you could set a band up miles and miles – so to speak – away from each other, so separation was good. We never used all twenty-four tracks with the basic recording of *Bomber* because we always needed to have a few tracks left over for overdubs. I probably used about ten tracks for drums on that album, one for the bass, one for the guitar and for the initial guide vocal – that would be tracking for the song's backing. Then we'd just continue overdubbing on any given song so, for instance, Lemmy's lead vocal and then perhaps two or three tracks for harmonies, which we'd then bounce down to one track and Eddie definitely had a few for his lead guitar overdubs. With Motörhead being a three-piece band, there wasn't call for too many overdubs.'

The band played at a volume that threatened to break the sound barrier, guitarist 'Fast' Eddie Clark explained in an interview with www.hardradio.com. 'It wasn't our fault... I was for ever trying to hear myself. So I was for ever adding fucking amps over my side, and Lemmy was just adding more and more on his side, and then Phil had bigger monitors – see what I mean? I mean, there were times… your ears would shut off. And all you got with it was this *bzzz*, and you had to just kind of look around and watch Phil and what his hands were doing, just trying to keep a *where are we*? You'd be thinking, I'll watch his hands and hopefully I'll know roughly where we are. It was one of those. But each one of us, because we never really interfered with each other's stuff, I let Lemmy get on with his and Phil get on with his and vice versa. So I'd be over my side trying to hear what I wanted to by adding more and more stuff. And, of course, they'd be doing the same over on their side. It was like, "Hey, guys, why don't we try turning down and starting again?" It was too late for that.'

Beginning with 'Fast' Eddie Clarke and Lemmy's guitar and bass rigs, engineer Trevor Hallesy recalled, 'On Eddie's stack, I would have used a 58 mic up close but was trying to get a bit more ambience for the room mic. I used a Neumann 84 mic on Lemmy's amp, which was the same Marshall 4 x 12 he'd used on *Overkill*, and I remember Lemmy used a five-string bass on one track on *Bomber*. I also remember putting heavy-ambience mics on the drums and using those valve microphones on the drum overheads but I also remember, in the mix, we didn't use that much of the ambient mics because they were too ambient, it was too live and was taking away from the power of the drums really.

'I was using similar mics as I had at Roundhouse but we did use a few more valve microphones, which we didn't have at Roundhouse. They are old microphones that don't have transistors and require a separate valve power supply to drive them. They're much warmer and, in addition to the warmth, have a certain charm to them that transistors didn't have. Motörhead wasn't traditionally the band you'd notice using a valve microphone on because they're a heavy rock band so you want that sort of edge and toughness, where valve microphones tended to soften things down. But they were still nice on vocals, even on Motörhead, because they can make a vocal sound very warm and real.'

When attention turned to tracking Lemmy's vocals, 'I used a valve mic on the vocals, instead of a standard transistor 87,' says Hallesy. 'I believe it was a Neumann Valve 64, which was a very warm-sounding mic. I actually ended up buying one shortly afterwards.' While Lemmy again handled the majority of the album's lead vocals, he recalled in his autobiography that 'Bomber is… the one album where Eddie sings a track, "Step Down". He'd been bitching that I was getting all the limelight, but he wouldn't do anything about it. I got sick of him complaining, so I said, "Right, you're gonna fucking sing one on this album." "Oh no, man," he protested, "I can't sing, man. I don't fucking got no voice…" "You're a perfectly good singer, man, get on the fucking microphone." So he did it with much grumbling. And it was like pulling teeth.'

In spite of that slight bump in the recording road, overall, engineer Trevor Hallesy felt 'everyone knew what they were doing and we took about three weeks to record, then mixed it at the Roundhouse.' About moving back to the familiar surroundings of his base with his beloved Cadac console, Hallesy recalled that the biggest challenge in mixing *Bomber* arose out of the fact that 'obviously, the sound I was getting at Olympic was different because of the live room, so I was compensatting for that a little with the EQ, maybe not putting quite so many delays and things, and using a bit of the natural ambience from Olympic on *Bomber*, as compared to *Overkill*.'

Bomber was completed on 31 August 1979 and Lemmy seemed to feel that – following almost four years of struggling – 'we were on a roll with two hit albums and knew we were on the rise, we were on our way'. The band's fans and critics alike appeared to agree, with an ever-growing legion of fans throughout the country sending the band's third studio album all the way to UK No. 12 and spawning UK No. 34 hit single 'Bomber' as well as fan favourites 'Dead Men Tell No Tales' and 'Stone Dead Forever'.

Billboard magazine would later celebrate in their review of the album the undeniable fact that 'the music here on *Bomber* explodes on song after song, thanks to the crazed performances of the aforementioned band members as well as the well-overdriven, ear-rattling production perfection… A top-shelf Motörhead album, one of their all-time best, without question… its best moments are as superlative as any Motörhead would ever record. The band was really on fire during this point in time and could seemingly do no wrong.' Lemmy, in his autobiography, seemed to agree that 'overall, *Bomber* was a really good record… "Bomber", "Stone

Dead Forever", "All the Aces" – those were great. "Lawman" was a weird pace for us, that was quite nice. *Bomber* was basically the transition record between *Overkill* and our next record, *Ace of Spades*, and that was its function really. And it peaked at No. 11 on the charts, so it got us up another notch success-wise.' Indeed, Motörhead would next have a breakout US hit with *Ace of Spades*, an album still considered by most to be the seminal blueprint for what would become the highly successful speed-metal genre for the 1980s, as Motörhead's legend continued to thrash the metal masses.

Chapter Four

Ace of Spades: 1980

Lemmy – bass, lead vocals
'Fast' Eddie Clarke – guitar, lead vocals on 'Emergency'
Phil 'Philthy Animal' Taylor – drums
Producer – Vic Maile
Released – 8 November 1980
Peak Chart Position: UK No. 4; 'Ace of Spades' peak position: UK No. 15

Rolling Stone would call Motörhead's seminal *Ace of Spades* 'gargantuan' upon release and that's precisely what the album represented in terms of both its sound and implications for the band, commercially speaking, as the 1980s began. Written and recorded in the year of its release, the album's success, according to Lemmy, represented 'a fairly brave new world, as we'd only done three albums before that, you know'.

Having come off the two-LP collaboration with Jimmy Miller, the band chose to enter the studio with a new producer to track *Ace of Spades*, with Lemmy recalling how he'd worked with Vic Maile with Hawkwind. 'He'd produced a couple things for us and he used to work for the Pye Records mobile studio, and he came up and did a Hawkwind thing, so I thought he'd be a good idea for Motörhead as well.' As Lemmy explained in his autobiography, 'We were at Jackson's Studios in Rickmanworth for about six weeks, from the beginning of August 1980 until mid-September.'

In describing the band's songwriting process on the record, Lemmy revealed that there was 'no pre-production process for that, we just write the songs, that's it. We typically write the music ahead of going into record but I always do a lot of the lyrics in the studio. Songwriting for me happens all different ways, you know, sometimes you get the music first, sometimes the lyrics. You always hear a melody in your head that works for the chorus and then give it a set of chords.' Going in-depth for an interview with *Inked* magazine, Lemmy recalled, 'I was in the studio writing them. All of them really. That's where I do my best stuff – panicked, under the clock, with people going, "Hurry up! Hurry up! We've only got two hours left!"'

From a production standpoint, 'Fast' Eddie Clarke recalled in the Classic Album DVD interview that '*Ace of Spades* became a little more of a production album'. Offering fans insight into Vic Maile's production style, Lemmy quipped, 'He was an asshole. He was really fucking dry and sarcastic. I remember Eddie had played this solo and he went, "Yeah, swell, wasn't that great?" And Vic replied, "Is that really your best shot?" Vic was definitely the best producer we ever had for that period and line-up.'

Drummer Phil Taylor added, in an interview for the band's tour programme, of working with the producer, 'Vic got me singing instead of just shouting all the time and he got me playing more solid,' while guitarist 'Fast' Eddie Clarke added, in the same band interview, that he enjoyed working with Maile on the album because, sonically-speaking, 'you can finally hear everything that's going on'.

Lemmy himself added, in the band's Classic Album interview, 'Most bands need somebody who's not in the band and not attached to the band, and who nobody in the band knows to sit there and be an asshole, they do.' In the same interview, Clarke said, 'Vic had a way of getting stuff out of us because he was too small for us to ever pop at. So he used to use that against us in a way and could get us to do almost anything.'

Recording commenced on 4 August with the band tracking live off the floor, as usual. Lemmy explained that the band's recording routine 'with any of our songs, in the studio, was we just play it and move on'. Lemmy said, '[I] played my Rickenbacker bass on that album, which was modified because I had Thunderbird pickups on it, which I liked because they had a single bar, so you got an even, thick tone to it, so that each string was the same volume. A lot of these new basses, sometimes you get one string that's louder than the others. It's a pain in the ass. I used to like those pickups because they were so powerful too, fuckin' really loud, you know? I was using standard old 1970s amps on that album.' While most bassists play to a drummer's groove, locked together in the pocket, Lemmy's unique style was unique. 'I've never played to the drums really, as a bass player. Sometimes when you write different songs, you do different things. Sometimes I play to the drums, yeah, but not that much. I tend to play to the vocals really. Eddie, Phil and I all played as separate players really, all trying to outdo the other ones, you know, in competition.'

Elaborating from a bandmate's perspective on that unique bass sound, Eddie Clarke explained, for Classic Albums, 'Motörhead wasn't a straightforward outfit to play with because, with Lemmy's bass playing being the way it was, it made us slightly different from all the other bands you'd hear at the time because there was no real bass guitar, it was like a bass rhythm.' Clarke, commenting in an interview with journalist David L Wilson on how his guitar-playing style complemented Lemmy's bass, said, 'The Stratocaster was more for Motörhead because Motörhead was such a raunchy kind of a sound that I needed something to kind of cut through but the Les Paul has always been my thing. You know that is where I came from, Eric Clapton – John Mayall sort of thing.'

On the inspiration behind the writing on the album's

title track, Lemmy began by reasoning that 'the rock'n'roll lifestyle is bound to influence Motörhead's themes and topics, I suppose, because I write all the lyrics. I used to play a lot of the one-armed bandit gambling games in England – luckily, you can't do it as much in California or I'd be broke – and I was spending a lot of money on it because they have them in all the pubs in England. So it was just about the gambling thing in general really. "Ace of Spades" was a word exercise on gambling.' Elaborating in his autobiography, the singer explained, 'I used gambling metaphors, mostly cards and dice. When it comes to that sort of thing, I'm more into the slot machines actually but you can't really sing about spinning fruit and the wheels coming down. Most of the song's just poker really: "I know you've got to see me/Read 'em and weep… Dead man's hand again… Aces and eights" – that was Wild Bill Hickock's hand when he got shot.' Expanding even further in the Classic Albums interview, Lemmy joked that listeners 'probably think it's all kind of clever metaphors, which it isn't, it's just a gamble to see if you can do a word exercise and fit all this gambling motif into these three verses.'

Once he'd completed work on the song's basic structure, 'me and Eddie and Phil all tinkered with it,' recalls Lemmy. Of the song's musical composition, Clarke shared with fans in the band's Classic Albums interview that 'originally *Ace of Spades* was going to be in based in A but I don't think Lemmy was particularly happy with it, because he wanted it to be based in E, so we switched it and it's the same sort of tempo, and fits within the same framework.' Lemmy recalled that during the song's recording that producer Vic Maile 'had us play wooden blocks. You can hear them on the "Ace of Spades" track, wooden blocks being slapped together with echo on them, all sorts of old Beatles musician tricks.'

Delving into the writing and recording of another of the album's classic tracks, '(We Are) The Road Crew', Lemmy mused, 'I think we got "(We Are) Road Crew" in ten minutes. We were at the studio and Vic said, "Go ahead and write some lyrics," and I wrote the lyrics in ten minutes and said, "OK, I've got it."' Once recording on the song commenced, Lemmy said in his autobiography that his 'chief memory of "(We Are) The Road Crew" is Eddie lying on his back in the studio, helpless with laughter, his guitar feeding back all over the place, halfway through what was supposed to be his solo. And we left it on because it was so fucking funny.'

Of 'The Chase is Better Than the Catch', Lemmy tells fans that the riff 'was one of Eddie's, I think, and the lyrics are self-explanatory really. It wasn't a difficult song to write, it was quite easy. I think we recorded it in one day.' In the band's Classic Albums interview, Eddie Clarke recollected of 'Jailbait', 'It's a rare one for us because it's in G. We did try to get away from A and E... obviously a lot of the keys you get stuck in.' In the same interview, drummer Phil Taylor shared his feeling that it was 'a good sound Eddie had on that guitar. Basically, I was trying to figure out where I could play double kick drums,' while Lemmy himself, in the course of the same discussion, clarified the song's lyrical content. To no one's surprise, '"Jailbait" is a song about the younger members of our entourage.'

Upon completion of principle tracking and mixing at the end of August 1980, Lemmy was 'great with it when it was done'. In his autobiography he explained that '*Ace of Spades* was one of our longer albums, in terms of the recording process. It went easier than our previous albums because we were on a roll and we couldn't be stopped then... because the band's popularity had been building – *Bomber* did better than *Overkill* and *Ace of Spades* promised to do even more. We were on our way up and we knew this one was going to be a hit. We felt good. I didn't realise then how doomed we were. It was the end of something really, instead of the beginning... Vic was a great man and a great producer, really brilliant... *Ace of Spades* was the ultimate record for that particular line-up of Motörhead.'

Released 8 November 1980, *Ace of Spades* was Motörhead's commercial break-out LP, establishing them as one of the UK's hottest metal acts. 'We were definitely on a roll then...' recalls Lemmy. 'The last two albums had been higher than each other on the charts. UK No. 27 and the other one got to UK No. 12, so we knew we were going to do all right. *Ace* got to UK No. 4 but we never did anything in America with that album. I don't even think we had a record deal in the US at that point. It wasn't even released. The first thing we ever released in the States was *Live at Hammersmith* and that was only after it had been UK No. 1.'

Elaborating in the band's Classic Albums interview, he said, 'We couldn't go wrong that year. I think we were on every poll and [in] every music paper. I think I only got beat on Sex Idol by David Coverdale.' As the band's popularity began to spill beyond the UK and into rock-hungry America, *Rolling Stone* announced their presence to the USA by excitedly declaring, 'This British trio plays with a brutish intensity that makes AC/DC seem like Air Supply. Granted, rock'n'roll as sonic shrapnel is a rather limited perspective but Motörhead offsets the music's relentlessness with surprisingly astute lyrics and exhilarating bursts of manic guitar. This is music for the thinking headbanger. Motörhead may actually be *too* intense for most American ears but, for the sheer adrenal rush of rock'n'roll, there's no one this side of The Clash who can touch them.'

Billboard, for its own part, enthusiastically concluded, 'With the 1980 release of *Ace of Spades*, Motörhead had their anthem of anthems – that is, the title track, the one trademark song that would summarise everything that made this early incarnation of the band so legendary, a song that would be blasted by legions of metalheads for generations on end. It's a legendary song, for sure, all 2 minutes and 49 bracing seconds of it. And the album of the same name is legendary as well, among Motörhead's all-time best... This singular sound (still loud and in your face, rest assured), along with the exceptionally strong songwriting and the legendary stature of the title track, makes *Ace of Spades* the ideal Motörhead album... *Ace of Spades* rightly deserves its legacy as a classic.'

Chapter Five

No Sleep 'til Hammersmith/ Iron Fist: 1981/1982

No Sleep 'til Hammersmith (1981)

Lemmy – bass, lead vocals

'Fast' Eddie Clarke – guitar, backing vocals

Phil 'Philthy Animal' Taylor – drums

Producer – Vic Maile

Released – 27 June 1981

Peak Chart Position: UK No. 1

'Motörhead' peak position: UK No. 6

Iron Fist (1982)

'Fast' Eddie Clarke – guitar, co-producer

Lemmy (Ian Kilmister) – bass, vocals

Phil 'Philthy Animal' Taylor – drums

Will Reid – producer

Released – 17 April 1982

Peak Chart Position: UK No. 6

Prior to entering the studio to record the highly anticipated follow-up to *Ace of Spades*, Motörhead would issue their first live album, the seminal *No Sleep 'til Hammersmith*. Released on 27 June 1981, it hit UK No. 1 to give the band their first taste of topping the charts.

It reflected their ever-growing popularity and established, as Lemmy views it, the 'template for live albums since. That album is truly live. I only overdubbed a couple of vocals for it. It did a pretty good job of reflecting Motörhead's energy live.'

Eddie Clarke, for his own part, explained in an interview with his official website that he felt the album was such a landmark event in metal because of 'the whole Motörhead attitude, what we kind of stood for back in those days. I used to think the show had a lot to do with it, having the bomber and stuff like that, and generally being so fucking loud you couldn't hear yourself think, but obviously you can't include that on the record. So I think it is just the thought that somehow we did capture that as well. The kids and everybody who was a fan of Motörhead used to enjoy the live gigs so much that a live album sort of takes them back there. So they get a little piece of the magic of the gig. Because our gigs were kind of special. Obviously the sound used to vary because of the volume and stuff but it was always a good show, you know what I mean?

'We had sold about 150,000 or 200,000 of *Ace of Spades* here in Britain. And I mean, in this country that's pretty good. It was our peak time. The bummer about the album

No Sleep 'til Hammersmith was that we were in America when it came out and it went straight to No. 1. And normally you'd be in the fucking pub and in the clubs, right? Everybody'd be buying you drinks. But, of course, we weren't there. Typical Motörhead. We were in America doing some stuff with Ozzy.'

Lemmy explained in an interview with Clarke's official website, 'We knew that *No Sleep* was gonna do well because people had been waiting for a live album from us for three years, but never in our wildest dreams did we think it would go straight in at No. 1... Actually, I was more pleased when *Ace of Spades* went in at No. 4 because *No Sleep* was a one-off. That said, it was also our death-knell because you can never follow a live album that goes straight in at No. 1. What are you gonna do, put out another one?'

The band took a brief break from the road – just long enough to record a new studio album. Album co-producer Will Reid quickly realised that the recording of the next studio album would take place under circumstances that were anything but relaxed. Success was all very well but it brought demands that were enough to stretch even a band whose mode naturally ran incredibly fast. 'Both *Ace of Spades* and *No Sleep 'til Hammersmith* had preceded *Iron Fist*, and had both been big albums for them,' recalls Reid. 'They'd sort of cracked it with those two – certainly as far as the UK was concerned – so they needed to make another album and were going to go on tour. We were a bit rushed and were given, I think, more or less three weeks to do the whole record. Management was like, "You *have* to finish it by this date, otherwise we won't get the album out and they'll be nothing to promote the tour with." So it was a bit pressured.'

And that pressure was only increased for Eddie Clarke – who added co-production duties to his guitar-playing responsibilities for the album. It was a decision which Lemmy came to regret, recalling in an interview years later that 'having Eddie produce it was a mistake that even he would now probably admit to'.

Clarke insists it was something he'd have put his hands up to on day one. 'I swear on my mother's grave, I didn't want to produce *Iron Fist*!' he declared in an interview with his own website. 'I'd produced the first Tank album [*Filth Hounds of Hades*, 1982] and producers all wanted ten or twenty grand – from a band that were on two hundred quid a week. Why should we pay some cunt that? I didn't want to play and produce. But Doug Smith was for ever telling us the band was skint and Lemmy's whole attitude was, "Let's let fucking Fancy Bollocks do it, he's just done the Tank album."'

Lemmy didn't quite see it that way. 'Eddie came to us and said he wanted to take a shot at producing,' he maintains. 'And, like idiots, we let him.'

Still, looking back, producer Will Reid felt, 'as a production team, Eddie and I were quite a good blend. Eddie was quite forward thinking in what he wanted to do in the studio and quite willing to experiment and, from an engineer's point of view, that's always a good thing to be able to do. I think we hit it off and there was no big ego thing. When we'd made the Tank record he'd relied on my experience to sort of relay what he wanted to do and the technical thing we'd do together, and any artistic things we might do together. For arrangements, he did most of that and so we worked well together. When we'd gotten to the Motörhead record, it was slightly different because he was actually playing on it, whereas in Tank he wasn't playing, so it had been easier for him to sit back and look at things more objectively maybe.'

Adding to the problems imposed by the tight schedule was the fact that Reid wasn't able to get into The Who's Ramport Studios, where he was resident engineer. 'That was a great studio for heavy metal and rock stuff, it just worked. But we had to work with the deadline and had to stick to the timescale, and had it mapped out: we have to have this done by then, this done by then, mixed by the end of the third week, or whatever it was. The band, at that time, were all living in one house together, about three or four miles from the centre of London, and Ramport Studios was just up the road, about a mile from where they were all living, which was another reason we wanted to do it at Ramport.

'As it turned out, the studio had been booked over that period by somebody else, so we had to find a studio and the one they picked was Morgan Studios, which was right up on the other side of London. At that point, I was living in south-east London and Morgan was virtually diagonally opposite it, so that meant driving right across London every day to get to the studio. So what I would do in order to get the band there on time was to drive by their house, pick them up and take them there every day. Lemmy would normally be at the pub already, so we would have to go pick him up from the pub on the way. That was pretty much how it went.'

Upon entering Morgan Studios to begin recording *Iron Fist*, the producer started 'recording the band on an MCI console and we recorded in Studio 1, which had a really big live room but the control room was upstairs, so you looked down on the live room where the band was recording from above. It was a little weird but like Abbey Road Studios. The control room itself was kind of long and narrow, it was a strange room.' With no time to waste, Reid had to make sure the basic tracks went down pretty quick. 'The drums and bass went down together and Eddie would have done a guide guitar track, then replaced those in overdubs. Phil and Lemmy didn't really want to hang around much for anything else and Lemmy was pretty keen to get down to the pub or something like that, so their tracks went down pretty fast as they were also pretty well-rehearsed before entering the studio.'

Lemmy: 'Me and Phil, I mean Phil was never in the studio for that album and we just didn't get it together, man, as you say.' Phil Taylor got down to drum tracking and Will Reid recalls he was 'a great drummer and a good time keeper, and didn't make a huge amount of mistakes. Phil's drums were up on a riser so, when I miked it up, I used a Sennheisser 421 on the kick drum and possibly a 57, the overheads were Neumann U-87s. What I'd started to do around that time was follow this technique that [premier-league producer] Glyn Johns had developed of recording drums with basically just three mics, a bass drum and two overheads. And the blend you get from positioning them the way he did was a nice sort of balance, so what I used to try and do was use that technique but then boost it up by having snare mics and tom mics just to add a bit of fullness to it. So I would have miked the toms in between the floor and rack toms with a Sennheisser 421 and on the snare I would have used a Sennheisser 441, generally I would have used that.'

When recording Lemmy's bass tracks, Reid quipped, 'Eddie had warned me before we started that Lemmy doesn't like a lot of bass on his bass guitar because when he plays it it's more like a rhythm guitar. So it makes it very difficult to get a blend of the three of them if you can't get that bottom end on it. Vic Maile managed it quite well on the records he did but I felt I never really got that drive from the bottom end – even if you've got that top end going as well, there is a blend of the two. But I think with Lemmy so insistent that "I don't want to hear any bass on my bass guitar", while there is some bass on it, I would have preferred it a little fuller myself. I miked Lemmy's cabinet with Shure 57s, that's what I tended to use in those days.'

As attention turned to tracking Clarke's guitar tracks,

Lemmy now feels that it wasn't fair to be saddling him with both production and performing duties 'and more than he could chew, anyway, to be in the control room and playing guitar in the other room. It's not possible really, we shouldn't have let him.' Nevertheless, in the moment, Will Reid recalled the pair negotiated that delicate balance by having 'Eddie play all his parts from the control room, that's generally how we would do it and I'd run him out from there into his amps. With Eddie's guitars, we would have doubled up all the rhythm guitar tracks, so Eddie did everything twice and he's a great rhythm player, probably one of the best rhythm guitarists I've ever worked with. I can't think of many – possibly apart from Pete Townshend – who are better than Eddie.

'Eddie was a very good riff writer, his riffs were classic. He didn't often make mistakes, generally got a pretty good sound, and can play the same thing again and again, so doubling up his guitars was a piece of cake. Eddie had a Marshall amp and I would have miked him with a combination of a 57 and 87 and then something further back, maybe another 87 to give it a bit of ambience. On his lead parts, we would sometimes go through a little Rockman pre-amp, then tape the output from the pre-amp as well, to give it a bit more fullness on the lead sound. Eddie tended to spend more time on his solos because he was a very competent rhythm player and, although he was a great lead player when he was in the mood, I think he'd be the first to admit that he didn't like playing lead as much as the rhythm stuff. But because he was the only guitar player and would have to play a lead in every song, I think he would have liked more time sometimes because it didn't always come naturally unless, like I said, he was in an inspired mood.'

Once the pair turned their focus to tracking Lemmy's lead vocals, producer Will Reid recalled, 'Eddie and Lemmy had done most of the writing and, as far as I remember, the only thing that wasn't totally finished once we'd entered the studio were Lemmy's lyrics. I remember Lemmy writing lyrics in the studio, and remember one time where he had one set of lyrics and probably spent an hour singing the song, getting it right, then coming in and listening to it a couple of times and saying, "I really don't like those lyrics, I'm going to completely rewrite them," and he went off to the bathroom and rewrote them while he was in there. Then came out a bit later with a whole new set of lyrics, went out and proceeded to sing them. We did tend to put the vocal mic up above Lemmy's head because that's how he liked to sing and we used a Neumann 87. He was pretty quick with his vocal takes, maybe a warm-up or two to get going, and then we laid the songs out verse by verse and got the whole song within a few takes.'

As principle recording wound down, Reid recalled feeling that — in spite of the implied pressures of being a member of the band he was producing — 'Eddie never really held back on telling the band what he thought a take should sound like and they were pretty responsive. I think the idea was they wanted it to work and to get it done as quickly as possible, and figured Eddie had a pretty good handle on what it took. The studio side of that dynamic between Eddie and the band went pretty smoothly, fairly light-hearted "fuck yous" and things of that sort but there was always a bit of underlying tension because Eddie's quite an aggressive guy. He gets wound up about things and, when he gets wound up, he can be pretty impossible. That didn't usually happen in the studio but I can remember taking him home in the evening, or being back at their house and going in to have a beer, and their being some physical fights going on between Eddie and Lemmy, as far as I remember. So he could get pretty wound up but they kept it professional in the studio. They did take a fair amount of drugs and drink a fair bit, so there was always that thrown in as well but they were reasonably professional when we were working. They were there to record and wanted to get it done, and we knew we had a deadline and couldn't mess around, we just didn't have the time.'

The tremendous pace was maintained as the band moved into mixing the album. 'Eddie and I would work together on the mix,' says Reid. 'But what would generally happen was he didn't sit on my shoulder saying, "Do this or do that." He'd generally rely on my ability to get it up and running, and then just say, "Well, why don't we try a little bit of this or that, or nothing at all," and we'd play it back, and anyone in the band who wanted to make a comment would. Phil was fairly laid back about the whole process and I remember he was there a lot but I don't remember a huge amount of input as far as what should happen, Phil was just friendly and a very funny guy. Lemmy definitely chimed in with his opinion when he had one.' Still, Lemmy felt, in hindsight, that he hadn't spent enough time around for the mixing sessions on *Iron Fist*. 'We always had complete control in the studio, on every album, but would leave it to the producer in those days for the mix, then go in and approve the finished mix, whereas nowadays I like to be at the mix at the same time.'

Reid and Clarke dived headlong into a whirlwind mixing session. 'We probably mixed two or three songs a day,' believes Reid. 'My main struggle during mixing was to get the bass end to blend because you've got a bass drum in there but, if you've got nothing to sit in with it down at that bottom end, it's quite hard. So I certainly was attempting to get the bass end and yet keep the attack on the bass, that was one thing I do remember struggling with a bit. I did tend to mix with the guitars a bit more in the forefront – if you listen to the Thin Lizzy stuff I did, the guitars are quite prominent.

'Although I was a drummer as a player,' he continues, 'I *love* a good rhythm guitar and that was a lot of the drive in Motörhead. So I would try to sit the guitars up front in the mix. At the end of the day, I was OK with the mix but there were a lot of things I felt we could have done better really. It was just the pressure of having to get it done, really, that I think took the edge off because that's a pretty quick time frame in which to do it, especially with as important an album as that should have been because of when it came in their career. I don't remember it being particularly long. In an ideal world, I wouldn't have recorded the album at Morgan because I didn't really like it but had no choice. It was out of my hands and all the people at the management and record companies wanted was a tape at the end of three weeks. All they wanted was a product.'

Commenting on those songs which he felt were stand-outs on the finished album, Lemmy's list was a short one. '"Loser" is not bad but there's a lot of songs on the record that didn't get done properly, like "Religion" and "Bang to Rights". There were five or six that I didn't like on the finished thing, where we should have spent more time on them and done them better.' Agreeing, producer Will Reid reasons that – in the context of past Motörhead albums – 'you also have to consider the songs themselves, which I don't think were quite as good as *Ace of Spades*. It was maybe, from their point of view, not their strongest record but it was sufficient. Collectively, we did OK and got it out on time given the deadlines we were working with. Given the different scenario and different timing, I would have, A, liked to have had more time and, B, recorded somewhere else – those would have been my two stand-out differences but I was very proud to be asked to do it. I think if you asked Eddie, he'd say there were he'd like to have done it differently or tried other things but it just wasn't the reality at the time. As far as working with the guys on that record, it was great, they were very good. They didn't really put any pressure on me, so working with Motörhead, I'd put it quite high on my list.' For Lemmy, the decision to choose 'Will as co-producer with Eddie on that album was ultimately a poor one on our part. Will Reid wasn't really a good producer, I don't think, not at that point – he got better later.'

Released on 17 April 1982, although the album peaked at UK No. 6, Lemmy felt *Iron Fist* didn't reflect the band as well as previous outings. 'We got complacent, was the problem with *Iron Fist*. We'd had three hits in a row and got complacent, and were riding along on the crest of the wave and didn't pay attention, and then they put that fucked-up cover on it while we were on tour in Europe and put it out with that fucked-up big plastic fist, fucking awful sleeve.' Critics weren't particularly fond of the album either, with *Billboard* magazine for one opining, '*Iron Fist* is mostly distinguished from its predecessors in terms of production and not favourably.' In commenting on the final product, in context of the band's greater catalogue, Lemmy seems to agree with his critics. 'I don't think we made any real turkeys,' he declares, 'apart from about half of *Iron Fist*.'

Fans also didn't respond as well to the album commercially but, arguably, the biggest fall-out for the band following the album's release came with guitarist 'Fast' Eddie Clarke's departure. Producer Will Reid believed that, in a way, the split occurred as a direct extension of his and Eddie's bond over co-production. That collaboration was scheduled to continue that summer with a recording session in New York. 'I was asked to record this session with Wendy O Williams and the Plasmatics,' explains Reid, 'which led to Eddie quitting the band. We were trying to record this song, which didn't really go anywhere because we were trying to record Motörhead with Wendy O Williams doing this version of "Stand by Your Man" and we set everything up and started recording, and when Wendy started singing it was really a disaster. You wouldn't have wanted to put your name on it, quite honestly.

'There was this sort of band meeting where Eddie said, "This really is a joke, why are we doing this?" Why don't we spend the time we've got booked here to record some other stuff? Bluesier and a slightly different avenue for the band, that Eddie wanted – and I think Phil as well – wanted to do. But Lemmy wouldn't have any of it and was quite keen on Wendy and wanted to do it. So Eddie basically said, "If that's the way it's going to be, then I'm out of it, I don't want to have anything to do with it," and said to me, "Come on, let's go," and I was really stuck and couldn't have really said "no" at that point, because I agreed with Eddie. I don't remember any physical stuff, but there certainly was quite a lot of verbal fighting.

'I remember I did one gig recording them live in Toronto at the beginning for their North American tour and Eddie quit shortly after that. The studio thing was really where it happened though. It all turned into a very difficult situation and I got stuck right in the middle of it, and Lemmy's always blamed me for that, which is sad really. I have read accounts of the fall-out where it was me and Eddie on the one side and he and Phil on the other, and the outcome of it really was that Eddie walked out. I was kind of with Eddie on the production side so I really had no choice but to go with him. I was a bit sad about that really.' In an interview with his official website years later, Clarke would explain, 'I still feel justified in saying that Wendy O Williams thing was a piece of shit and that we shouldn't have done it because *Iron Fist* hadn't gone down well and the tour had been a disaster. We needed something with a bit of credibility, not another fucking joke. Lemmy even suggested crediting it to Motörhead and Wendy O Williams with a disclaimer that it had nothing to do with Fast Eddie Clarke – well, that really fucking did me. It wasn't about me, it was about Motör-fucking-head.'

'Eddie used to leave the band about every two months but this time it just so happened that we didn't ask him back,' Lemmy explained in his autobiography. 'We didn't try to persuade him, which is why he stayed away – that surprised him a bit, I think. But we were just tired of him because he was always freaking out and he was drinking a lot back then… We had to get another guitar player fast so we could continue the tour and we chose Brian Robertson, who had been in Thin Lizzy. Technically, he was a better guitarist than Eddie but, ultimately, he wasn't right for Motörhead. The record we made with him, *Another Perfect Day*, was very good.'

Heading into 1983 and their next album, Motörhead quickly rebounded from the failure of *Iron Fist* with plans for that new album, with a new producer, rock veteran Tony Platt.

Chapter Six

Another Perfect Day: 1983

Lemmy – bass, vocals
Brian Robertson – guitar, piano on 'Rock It'
Phil 'Philthy Animal' Taylor – drums
Producer – Tony Platt
Released – 4 June 1983
Peak Chart Position: UK No. 20

Following the commercial failure of *Iron Fist* and the departure of guitarist 'Fast' Eddie Clarke, Motörhead were in a period of rebuilding when they entered the studio to record the ironically titled *Another Perfect Day*, with Lemmy explaining the decision to hire Thin Lizzy guitarist Brian 'Robbo' Robertson as one rooted in the fact that 'Phil Taylor is a big Thin Lizzy fan, so was I, but I wouldn't have picked

Robbo. Phil said, "Oh, come on, let's get Robbo," so I said, "All right," and gave him a shot.

'Eddie left us in the middle of the tour in America, and we were stuck in a hotel in New York and didn't have a guitar player because the last show Eddie had done was at the Paramount. We didn't audition anybody because we were in a hurry and had already cancelled four or five shows, I think, so we had to replace him with another guitarist quickly. Robbo was the only one available and flew over, and we had one day's rehearsals and were on the road again.'

Benefiting from a breaking-in period of sorts on the road to gel as a re-formed trio, drummer Phil 'Philthy' Taylor revealed some of the musical inner workings of that process in an interview with the band's biggest online fansite, explaining that 'once Lemmy starts playing, he's sort of out there on his own, in a way. It's something that came naturally; but when Robbo joined the band, we started working it out a bit more. When Eddie was with the band, I played more with the guitar than I did with Lemmy because he's not really a bass player. Lemmy always plays so fast that it's always been down to the guitarist and me to keep the rhythm and melody going. Lemmy is just non-stop playing all the time so, for the highs and lows of the numbers, the ups and downs, light and shade – whatever you want to call it – it's basically down to Robbo and myself. I'd never played much before, so it's probably a lot more difficult for Robbo than for me.

He'd always played in bands that had a proper bass player, so to speak.'

Robbo, speaking with surprising candidness for his own part in the same interview, recalled his decision to join the band. When people asked, 'What are you doing joining Motörhead?' he said, 'I didn't say I like them. I hate Motörhead. But I respect them for playing shit for so many years and making money at it. And they're original. I won't say Lemmy's a very good bass player but he's very original. Lemmy is Lemmy. And I know my style is very forceful and always has been.'

Recalling the stylistic changes in the band that came with the guitarist's addition to the line-up, Lemmy explained, 'Robbo was a great blues guitarist but he made us more pop,' while the album's producer, Tony Platt – the right-hand man to Mutt Lange throughout the late 1970s – added, 'I thought very much so [that] Robbo brought something new to the band.' Detailing his pre-production process with the band prior to entering the studio, Platt explained, 'We rehearsed everything at Noma's [rehearsal studios], quite a bit of time rehearsing and came out, actually, with a set of reasonably coherent demos, from the boombox in the room. Some pre-production, actually, was getting them to jam a bit and see what came out from that. Somewhere I've still got loads of cassettes of all this stuff we jammed and mucked around with. Sometimes, after everybody went off to the pub, Robbo and I might mess around with overdubbing little bits of guitars on these jams just to see where they went, so there was quite a bit of that. It was a very creative process that we went through.'

Lemmy: 'We wrote the songs the same way – me and Phil and Robbo in the rehearsal room, and writing with Robbo versus Eddie was more or less the same, he pulled his weight there.'

Perhaps not surprisingly, in the context of looking back to the album's recording, Lemmy feels 'Robbo did a good job, I just thought he could have been more for the band and less for Robbo'. Producer Tony Platt revealed that, during pre-production, 'a large proportion of what I was finding myself having to do was manage the relationship between Lemmy and Robbo, that started right from pre-production. Lemmy doesn't really operate as a dictator, he sort of defies description in a way because he's a very intelligent bloke who just likes playing loud music really fast. It's almost a simplistic lifestyle he's chosen for himself and, in that respect, I think the idea of a three-piece band and the camaraderie that brings is the simplest possible form of making loud rock music. So I don't think it was a matter of Lemmy being a control freak or Robbo not being an equal band member, it's just there was a widening chasm of operating methods that opened up as time went on during the album's recording.

'Having worked with Mutt Lange, I was very much in the idea that pre-production is really important. I *still* think it's very important. And knowing what you're going to do before you go into the studio is very important. It's always been very important for me as well to have experienced a live performance of a band before heading into the studio, to see what it is that gets everybody going and hear what gets everybody going, so that I can kind of build up a picture of where we ought to be going with the album. That was considerably more difficult where Motörhead was concerned because their time keeping isn't great in terms of turning up… just being there when they're supposed to be. So things were kind of drifting a little from time to time.'

Aside from the band's remaining consistently loud from gig to gig, when his research and pre-production were complete, heading into the studio the producer felt that 'the whole set-up was quite different in respect to Robbo being in there from the way Motörhead had been before with Eddie Clarke because that was much more of an anarchic situation. I'd been to a couple of Motörhead gigs and one of the things I'd discovered – being an engineer and wanting to protect your ears – quite often those gigs were pretty much too loud for me. I discovered that when I put my fingers in my ears I could hear all the harmonics that were going on and all of the melodies that were going on underneath. And I found that absolutely fascinating because, if you just kind of wander into a Motörhead gig and you're more of a rock fan, you'd probably go, "Wow, that's just a lot of noise really." It's the sound power that gets a lot of people going but, in actual fact, there's a whole load of stuff going on underneath that's really a lot more sophisticated.'

Using that sonic realisation to assist in mapping out

Another Perfect Day's production blueprint, Platt further called on his experience 'working with Mutt Lange on *Highway to Hell* and *Back in Black* prior to my work with Motörhead, where some of the things I brought to the engineering on those AC/DC records were techniques that I was always working with and developing in any case. With Motörhead records, I think they are actually better than most in terms of that power that they have live being generated on record. But quite often it's not the sort of power that you get when you're not listening loud – you have to turn them up. One of the things which I think we started to achieve on *Highway to Hell* and we definitely achieved on *Back in Black* is it's a record that still sounds as ballsy if you play it quiet as if you play it loud. And I've heard it on systems all over the world. I think my biggest buzz ever was walking into Madison Square Garden before a Van Halen concert and they were doing the sound check and running the PA up, and I walked into the arena literally as the sound guy was putting "Back in Black" on, and the hairs went up on the back of my neck hearing that played over such a big system. The clarity of it was still there, that was the thing – it wasn't just loud, it was loud and clear. And I think *Another Perfect Day* has that clarity of sound and power.'

Detailing some of the technical aspects of the studio where team Motörhead recorded *Another Perfect Day*, the producer recalled, 'Olympic Studios, where we recorded the album, had this Raindirk console that we recorded on.

Olympic Studios used to have Helios consoles, which was the console I learned on and that we mixed *Highway to Hell* on – the Bob Marley stuff was done on that. But by then they had put in a Raindirk, which was essentially not that different from a Helios. It was essentially the next generation of that console. It was a 24-track analogue machine we were recording on but I think we might have gone to a slave reel.

'In any case, 48-track recording was possible by then and what I had got into doing was to record the basic track, then make a slave reel and put the original away so that we weren't continuously playing the backing track master and wearing it out. So you maintained the integrity of that original master because every time it goes past the head you lose a little bit of oxide, which is not a good thing. So that tended to be my standard preference.'

They entered Olympic Studios in February 1983 to begin formal work on the album. 'There's a sort of interesting addendum to this because I'd worked with Lemmy before then on a track called "White Line Fever",' Platt remembers, 'in a studio on the south coast of England, so I'd had a little bit of experience of the early days of Motörhead. This was kind of returning to something.' One big difference the producer would soon discover was in maintaining that peace between Lemmy and Robbo. 'It's very true that a producer is a psychologist as much as anything else but, to be honest, none of those things would really ever work with someone like Lemmy. He's probably several steps ahead of anything like that. He's a very straightforward guy. I don't think I would have tried to pull stunts on him at all because I had – and still have – more respect for him than that. It was really more "let's get on with this, let's do this as good as we can and see where we can go with it".

'Lemmy could get distracted in the studio. Some of the time he'd decide he'd had enough and wanted to go off to the pub, which he would do. I don't think Lemmy had a great deal of patience with the process of recording in terms of refining it; he's very workman-like, in terms of "let's get on with this and get this done". So there's a lot of that but, if there's a certain amount of refining to maybe take it to a different place, or push it a little bit further, I didn't find that he really had a lot of patience with that.

'I'm a great sort of "let's go on a voyage of experience and see where we can go" type motivator. It doesn't seem reasonable to me if a band has a new line-up and an opportunity, maybe, to push the frontiers and tread some ground they've not trodden before, that you would pass that experience up. To me, there would be no point in us trying to make a Motörhead album that sounded the same as it did with Eddie with Robbo because you might as well just have Eddie there. I think with Robbo the songs had more structure. Recording Robbo was very much a matter of having not really found out why Robbo was chosen to join the band and, therefore, just having to work with what was going on. I then took the positive, glass-half-full approach and thought, well, what advantage can we get from this set of circumstances? How can I push it in a positive direction?'

Lemmy, for his own part, felt the possibility of progress was hindered, in part, by the fact that 'there's so many guitars on that album it's unbelievable. My preference would have been quicker 'cause I'm impatient, I like things yesterday if possible and Robbo took so long it cost us thousands, that album. I don't know if Robbo was focused in the studio but he was a workaholic, all right.'

Agreeing, at least with the latter part of Lemmy's assessment, producer Tony Platt recalls of Robbo that he would 'just kind of get on with it, so he was getting a bit frustrated by the whole thing. The interesting dynamic, I think, that was in there was: if you'd looked at that again from the outside, you might have thought, why did Lemmy pick Robbo to join Motörhead? I still have no idea, Lemmy has never explained it. He's the only one who could possibly explain it because the whole essence of Robbo's guitar playing is melodic with a whole lot of "guitar-techy" type of approach to things.

'What Lemmy had been used to beforehand was just as loud and fast as you could get it. Then, when we got into the whole situation of Robbo wanting to develop the melodies and seeing a lot of ZZ Top comparisons going on there, he really wanted to push the songs a little bit further and perhaps get the record to be a bit more tuneful. And then there was a certain amount of pushing back in the other direction from Lemmy so, as the album went on, the war broke out.'

'Tony worked more with Robbo than with me and Phil; they'd stay for hours after we'd gone and then we had to listen to what they'd done the next day, which was sometimes really overblown,' says Lemmy. 'There's like twenty guitar tracks on "Marching to War" and you don't need twenty guitar tracks on any track, ever.' Platt had a different approach to recording, which resulted in the multiple stacks of guitar tracks. 'With Robbo,' says Platt, 'who has a totally different technique than Eddie, he's much more technical in a lot of respects, he liked to layer a lot more. For instance, on some tracks, we would create a couple guitar tracks that bounced off each other, like on "I Got Mine". So we did a bit of layering and changing the sound between sections, we did quite a bit of that. Rather than trying to just have one sound that fed all the way through, to maybe even change guitars or amps to get a different texture in different sections. For miking guitars, it's back to Neumanns again — I like U67s and U87s on guitars and used them on Robbo's rig.'

When attention turned to capturing Lemmy's bass sound to tape, the producer worked in contrast to the way the band had done things before. 'I wanted to get a bit more clarity into it without losing the power. In fact, the other thing that's kind of pertinent to this is, around the same time I'd done 'White Line Fever' with Motörhead, I also did a whole load of tracks with Thin Lizzy, before Robbo joined. These were a whole bunch of demos we'd done, and it was around the time that Gary Moore was leaving and Robbo was joining, so Phil Lynott had a particular set-up that he used. He used a similar bass to Lemmy, a Rickenbacker, but what he used to do was [record] a stereo bass. He'd take the two outputs and one of the outputs would go up through what was essentially a guitar set-up of 4 x 12 stacks, and the other would go through a big acoustic 360 stack. So all the bottom end came from one stack and all of the top end came from the other. Phil Lynott's sound was that combination of the two things. I kind of thought the best thing to do here was apply the same thing.

'Lemmy has a particular amp that he uses, which is a Marshall. What I did was stick a low-end stack up at the same time and record it side-by-side with his normal set-up, and put it on a separate track. So when I came to mix, I had the low-end bass content in there that I could feed in, which was perfectly in synch and didn't get messy there.'

Continuing, Platt recalls, 'We were about two thirds of the way through the album and Lemmy's Marshall started making some nasty noises and then kind of stopped working, and it was right at the end of a week before we were about to take a couple of days off. So I said to the guitar tech, "You need to go and get this fixed before we come back on Monday." So the guitar tech went off and came back on the Monday, and I asked, "Did you get it fixed?"' And he said, "Well, we tried a couple of other amps and it just didn't sound the same, just absolutely, totally different." So the guitar tech said he'd taken it to a guy and he'd opened it up and noticed there were all sorts of things that had been changed on it, so he worked it over quite nicely and put it all back the way it ought to be. And my heart sank and, of course, we plugged it in and it just sounded very gutless and ordinary, so the conclusion I came to was: over the years, various techs that worked with Lemmy had obviously modified little bits of the amplifier so that it became more and more the way Lemmy wanted it to be. So after that, we had the amp put back the way it was and there it was sounding good again.

'To mic Lemmy's bass, I used a pair of microphones, so I had a D20 on the low bass parts and a U47 mic on the higher bass part.'

As with all past albums the band had recorded, Platt set the band up to 'track live off the floor during recording. We were in the big room at Olympic Studios, so there was plenty of space for everybody. Lemmy had his bass stack in quite a large booth that was separated a bit from the room and the guitars were behind some screens, and then the drums were right in the middle.' Phil Taylor had an elaborate drum kit set-up but he has said in interview, 'It's not really that big, it just looks it because it's all chrome. The rototoms are up high because I have no other place to put them and I sit very low behind the kick. I'm not a tall person anyway so, even before I had the rototoms, unless you were in the balcony nobody could see me.'

Platt employed the full weight of his experience when it came to tracking Taylor to tape. 'One of the things I picked up from Mutt really – I used to do it automatically but I became a little bit more fixated on doing it – was getting the tom toms to be tuned within the chord in the key of the song. When you're putting all these frequencies together, what you don't want is to have them fighting with each other. So it means then tom toms can occupy a space within the whole sound that is there for them.

'So every time the floor toms get hit you get dissonance between the note on the floor tom and one of the notes on the bass. It actually takes up rather a lot of space in the mix and you lose a lot of clarity and, therefore, you lose a lot of punch and a lot of power. And with Motörhead, power is very much the thing.

'I don't necessarily have a standard set-up of microphones. How I always go about it is: I learned to record drums with three microphones – it was back in those days – so I still start from the point of view of trying to get the drum kit to sound good before you even put a microphone on it. So we made sure it was tuned, got rid of any nasties that were going on there, made sure the tom-toms were tuned, and well with the snare and the kick drum. Phil's a very good drummer and was very happy to kind of get stuck in and really get the drums to sound as good as possible. So that was the first thing and, once we got the drums sounding the way we wanted them to sound on the studio floor, I was then able to start miking up.'

Platt's next step in that process involved 'putting my overhead microphones, which are the ones that do a lot of the work and pretty normally are Neumann U87s. The thing about cymbals is that they don't comprise just top frequencies, so you actually don't want a microphone like an AKG-451 – is a bit too toppy for me for cymbals because it over-enhances the top end and doesn't really handle the low end. The substance of a cymbal, the harmonic carrier frequencies, are in the low area, so the U87 has the clarity to enable all of the harmonics of the cymbal to come through. When you put two of them up you get a very nice, precise stereo image from that and the phase is extremely good on those microphones, so it's all of those things that tend to lead me toward the U87s. Over the years I've tried lots of different overhead microphones, I've used AKG-414s, which I find a little bit too soft and the phase is not always that great on those so, for Motörhead, the U87 worked best.

'I used a condenser mic on the snare, which is perhaps a little more unusual because the tendency for rock music is for people to just use an SM57. I very much like Neumann KM86s or KM84s, partially because they are small enough to be able to get into the space you want to get into. Also because they have a ten-decibel pad on the microphone itself, so you can pad the mic down so it doesn't overload too much. I don't like the mic to be too close to the snare drum, so you can actually get the pop off it. There would have been an under-snare mic, which almost inevitably would have been an SM57.

'For the kick, there again it's slightly unusual because I have a tendency to go for a U47 on the kick drum. Again, you see, what I'm trying to do with a kick drum is to get the feeling of this large column of air moving. And the pattern of a U47 is particularly useful in that respect because it's got quite a bit of cardio impact, so you're not just getting this kind of tiny little "tick-tick-tick" in the middle of the kick drum. Also, you get a really good bass response from a U47 because you get a lot of those low-carrier sub-frequencies. In effect, using a U47, back in those days, kind of does the same thing as when people use a D112 and an NS10 speaker now, looking for that sub-bass thing. You can get that all on the U47 and I always liked that. Again, I liked the clarity of it and, I think, also because it's important that the sounds you're getting off the individual microphones fit into the texture and timbre of the sounds you're getting on the overheads. If you've got a completely different timbre happening on the kick drum to that which you're hearing in the kick drum in the overheads, you start having sounds fighting with each other. And what I'm trying to do, my feeling is that all of these spot microphones on the kit should be complimentary to the overall kit sound.'

The producer turned to working with Lemmy on the album's lead vocal tracks. 'The thing about Lemmy is the position he sings in is really important, with his head tilted upward – that's part of how he gets his sound. I seem to remember that I actually had an SM58 up and a condenser mic at the same time. It didn't really take that long to get Lemmy's vocals down – it took one or two takes. He knew what he was doing, the lyrics were all sorted and off he went. The lyrics were coming all the time and we went in with some tunes without the lyrics finished, definitely. I still to this day tell anybody who will listen that, as far as I am concerned, Lemmy's one of the best lyricists the music business has ever had. I think his lyrics are absolutely stunning – very clever, very funny and really, really well-crafted to fit with the songs. So there were a lot of elements where I felt, well, a lot could be done here.

'I'm not averse to writing in the studio and one of the things I definitely learned from Mutt is that songs can and should continually develop. And really what you're doing in the studio is you're pushing and pushing and pushing the song and sound and arrangement, and then, some point along the way, you say, "This is a really good representation of the song," and you click the shutter, and you have that snapshot, and that's the one that you keep.'

Throughout production the band's focus stayed primarily on navigating through what *Billboard* magazine later described as a collection of recordings that 'captures Motörhead mainstays Ian "Lemmy" Kilmister and "Philthy Animal" Taylor struggling to adapt their raw power and unparalleled distortion to Robertson's more mainstream hard-rock instincts and melodic tendencies.' It's a description that Tony Platt recognises. 'I'll admit there was a certain amount of intention to try and be able to get some of the songs playable on FM radio and, in that respect, to try and move outside just the kind of hardcore rock stations which will always play A*ce of Spades*. At that particular time, you had bands like ZZ Top coming through with songs that had a bit more structure to them and were perhaps more playable on the driving stations. So I think there was a little, in the back of my mind, well, it'd be cool if we could get a couple of tracks that could work in that context.'

Principal recording was not completed as quickly as it had been for the previous release. 'From pre-production through to the end of tracking we had about six weeks, so it wasn't a quick album.' But when everything had been taken down, Platt could turn his attention to mixing. 'I feel it's all part of the same process,' he believes. 'I think that when I'm recording I'm aiming for the mix and the mix is aiming for the mastering, so they're all kind of integral processes. Lemmy wasn't around much but Robbo was very interested in everything. He took a great deal of interest in everything and felt it was important to be part of the whole thing.

'When I'm mixing, I quite often, in rock stuff, use short delays to thicken guitars a little bit but I record guitars with at least two microphones on different speakers so that I get plenty of opportunity to spread the sound out across the stereo, rather than just being on sort of a pinpoint mono, and that was the case with Motörhead. With *Another*

Perfect Day, I was focusing on really just getting the mixes punchy with the clarity and power in there, and excitement – get it all across.'

Ultimately, in spite of its rollercoster of ups and downs in the studio, the producer had positive memories of the sessions. 'I really, really enjoyed making the album,' shares Platt. 'When we finished it, everyone was really pleased with it. Lemmy was really pleased with it and said so on a number of occasions. There was no doubt when we finished it that he seemed to like it. I'm still very proud of that album, think it's a good album and think it could have been better if it had gone a little more smoothly but still think it came out pretty damn good at the end of the day.

'In terms of favourites, I think "I Got Mine" was pretty good. I also think the guitars in "Dancing on Your Grave" are really quite cool, I like that too.' Lemmy, for his own part, commented in looking back on the experience that he 'liked the record. I thought it was a good album and a lot better than *Iron Fist* but our fans didn't like it. I think it was Robbo they didn't like because he was just weird and they didn't buy the album anyway because it was too much of a departure really, it wasn't as brutal. A couple of tracks were, like "Die you Bastard" and "Funny Farm" – they were old-true Motörhead songs but Robbo was a bit of a twiddler, you know – the solos were too long on some of the songs, I thought. All in all, though, I liked the album – it was five times the album *Iron Fist* was, I thought.'

The album was released on 4 June 4 1983 and reached

UK No. 20, and *Billboard* says that 'to this day *Another Perfect Day* remains one of the most unique (albeit misunderstood) albums in the entire Motörhead catalog… Thanks in part to Tony Platt's excellent production, *Another Perfect Day* ranks among the band's best-sounding records ever.' Still, the magazine went on to point to the fact that the album ultimately suffered from what was 'clearly a nervous musical marriage from the start… Robertson's unwillingness to be a team player (refusing to play standards like "Bomber" live, never mind his ridiculous fashion sense) virtually guaranteed his eventual sacking.'

Offering perhaps the most direct insight into why Robbo was ultimately sacked, Lemmy explains that while 'Robbo pulled his weight musically all the time, he was personally just wrecked out of his head all the time. He used to drink a bottle of whiskey before the sound check sometimes. On the first two tours he was excellent – we toured America, then Japan and he was great. Then when we toured Europe, he went off the rails and went nuts. He was a pain in the ass, you know, he didn't really want to be in the band. The last gig we did with Robbo, we did "Another Perfect Day", then he started it again and I said, "We've just done that," and he said, "I'm sorry," and started it a third time, so that was the final straw.'

Recalling the album in his autobiography, Lemmy said that, whatever anyone else thought, 'our fans hated it… They thought we were "going commercial". I think *Another Perfect Day* was a good change for us and maybe it was a mistake that we didn't experiment more earlier. Maybe we should have carried on in that direction... but not with Brian!'

Chapter Seven

Orgasmatron/Rock'n'Roll: 1986/1987

Orgasmatron (1986)

Lemmy – bass, vocals

Phil Campbell – guitar

Würzel – guitar

Pete Gill – drums

Producer and Engineer – Bill Laswell and Jason Corsaro

Released – 9 August 1986

Peak Chart Position: UK No. 21

Rock'n'Roll (1987)

Lemmy – bass, vocals

Phil Campbell – guitar, slide guitar on 'Eat the Rich'

Würzel – guitar, slide guitar on 'Stone Deaf in the USA'

Phil 'Philthy Animal' Taylor – drums

Producers – Motörhead and Guy Bidmead
Engineer – Guy Bidmead
Released – 5 September 1987
Peak Chart Position: UK No. 34

Regrouping Motörhead after the second departure of a guitarist in four years, Lemmy appeared to be opting for an insurance policy with the hiring of two guitarists. He commented on the decision in his autobiography. 'Finding a new guitar player wasn't a difficult process really. I just did an interview in *Melody Maker* in which I mentioned that we were going to get somebody unknown this time around and the applications flocked in. It was so simple, in fact, that we would end up choosing two guitarists... We liked both Phil Campbell and Würzel immensely... We couldn't decide between the two of them, so we had them both come back. The plan was to hold a battle of the guitarists to see which of 'em came out on top...

'The [day of the final audition] they were already talking over how to persuade me to take them both. But they didn't have to try because I'd been thinking along the same lines. A four-piece is a lot more capable of playing different stuff – with two guitar players you're bound to get that.'

Expanding further, in an interview with *Chart* magazine, Lemmy recalled that his decision to hire both was a matter of simply not being able to 'choose between them. They worked well together for a long time.' The line-up was augmented by drummer Pete Gill. 'Probably the first few months of when Phil and Würzel and Pete Gill joined, 'cause we seemed to be laughing all the fucking time, it was great. They took ten years off me because I was seeing it through their eyes and it was all new to them.'

Newly inducted drummer Pete Gill recalled of the opportunity to join one of Metal's most musically aggressive rhythm sections, 'It was great to play with Lemmy. He has a unique style and it demanded from me a very strict style of playing. I could have played around a lot more and put in lots of different fills but that would have clouded the issue, so I kept it very strict in both performance and time keeping, but I was always pushing Lemmy and the band to the limits, and it showed in our live performances. We were honestly on fire every night and, although exhausting, it was so, so rewarding.'

In his autobiography, Lemmy said, '*Orgasmatron* was our first full studio album in three years and the line-up, except for me, was completely different... but that didn't faze us any.' What would have fazed most bands – regardless of their inner comfort level as musicians – was the time frame in which the band had to record the album, with Lemmy revealing in interview – with an air of surprising ease – 'We made that record in eleven days, which, as you might have figured out by now, was no big deal for Motörhead. It was very easy, in fact, because the guys were so glad to be there.' Talking to the band's largest fansite, Lemmy later said that tight purse strings led to the tighter schedule. 'Actually, we didn't have the money to take a whole lot of time in the studio. Three years off didn't help things too much financially. We also got it done that quick... Even if we had done it ideally, it wouldn't have taken much longer.' They had to know what they were doing by the time they got in the studio. Gill explains how they did it. 'We rehearsed the album about twice a day for about two weeks so, when we hit the studio, we just really played it live and recorded it really fast – I think about two days for the drums.'

The band had settled on famed London recording studio Master Rock, equipped with the Focusrite Forte console designed by legendary Rupert Neve. It was one of only two in existence. The system 'was, and still is, considered by many as sonically the finest console ever built', according to the company's website. 'Renowned for upholding a level of sonic integrity beyond compare... The original 110 pre-amplifier topology forms the cornerstone of each channel... The benefits include superb common-mode rejection, an excellent overload margin and, with its shared gain structure, an extremely low noise floor and super-wide bandwidth... The original mic-pre used rotary-switched gain controls and high-quality audio transformers... The ISA 110 EQ (featuring the original Lundhal LL1538 transformer and bespoke Zobel network) and ISA130 compressor [were] the two key modules from this definitive analogue console.'

Opting to go with a new recording team, Lemmy chose avant garde producer Bill Laswell. 'We went in the studio with Bill... and his engineer, Jason Corsaro,' explained Lemmy in his autobiography. 'They'd just come over from the States and they didn't know us at all... Bill and Jason were being all gung-ho American. "Let's get it on, boys. It's gonna be great!"' Pete Gill adds, 'Because of Bill Laswell's background, I thought he saw us as a mighty challenge and some of the tracks on the album certainly bore his hallmark. He said I was one of the best players he had worked with – and that was a nice compliment! I think his thoughts on Lemmy and all of us was, Man, this is one hell of a beast... and I think before he met us that he didn't think we could play as well as we did.'

A noted bass player himself, Laswell explained in interview how he came to evolve his way of working in the studio. 'The whole idea of production and making records came out of... I think it was the necessity to control your own sound. I would play on things and it wouldn't sound the way I had imagined it or the way I even thought it originally sounded. So I think it was a need to establish a sound, my own individual sound and have a little more control on what the end result was in terms of mixing and creating music. Then you become interested in other sounds and how they relate, and that all moves forward to being able to make records... By opening up, just giving in to that and being free from a lot of things, you come into contact with something that can help you, that will give you these results. In other words, in a way, it's kind of saying that ignorance is very much a part of that. Because I'm not trying to know something or teach something or learn something and be about something. I'm trying to just get rid of everything and feel something and let it happen. I'm not saying "be stupid", I'm saying get away from the brain.' In interview with Anil Prasad, Laswell said, 'As far as bassists playing melody or rhythm, it comes down to whatever the project is. If someone is playing melodically great bass, that's a positive, I think. I'm more critical of acrobatics and not knowing how to create a feel or a memorable line.'

Lemmy, for his own part, says of the sessions, 'I played my Rickenbacker bass on that record, the one with the sticker "Born to lose, out to lunch" on it and I used the 412 with an amp for *Orgasmatron*.' He was particularly pleased with the title track. 'That's probably the best I've ever written, along with "March ör Die".' In a 1986 interview he said that the song's inspiration had nothing to do with the Woody Allen movie *Sleeper*, in which the main character experiences all the fun of a futuristic machine of the same name. 'Not at all,' said Lemmy. 'I never thought of that when I wrote it. Since then everybody's been coming up to me and mentioning that. I thought that I invented the term but maybe it was a subconscious thing.'

He explained the writing process in a website interview. 'There's one I wrote in my sleep. Got up in a hotel room at about four in the morning, wrote it down and got back into bed! Didn't even remember doing it. Probably my best set of lyrics too – which might say a lot!' In the same interview, he revealed that the song is about 'the three things that I hate most in life: organised religion, politics and war. Things like people that go to church and cum in their pants while communing with Jesus Christ. It's all a bunch of bullshit. If you are really into that, you don't need to go to a church to talk to God, you can talk to Him anywhere, you know? Or if you join a political party and get your jollies off of that when your party wins and all that. It's the herd instinct. The same thing with the war. They give you a nice new uniform and march you off to die.'

Songwriting, according to Pete Gill, 'usually was a four-way thing – except Lemmy always insisted on writing all the words, which was cool. Phil and myself would basically come up with the riffs – we wrote "Killed by Death" in about an hour. Lemmy came up with the riff on "Orgasmatron" and I initially thought it was very boring. I thought about putting in some off-the-wall drum patterns but then I just got into this really hypnotic groove and the feel became amazing and, although it is very, very repetitive, the tabloids always say it is their favourite track on the album. And it is my best playing, so I am not going to argue, but my own personal favourite is "Ace of Spades" – but I didn't co-write that. I wish I had!'

Crafting the title track's vocal in the studio was an unusual experience for Lemmy. He told Tom Headbanger, 'The only time I ever really tried to sing was on "Orgasmatron" and I gave up on it after that and went back to not giving a shit.' Pete Gill witnessed that business-like attitude in full flow. 'Lemmy would often write some lyrics literally minutes before he sang them.'

Lemmy approved of how things went in the studio. 'Bill did a good production,' he says. 'He just treated it like it was his band and not mine when he was mixing. During recording, he got a good bass sound and got a good guitar sound.' Sadly, when attention turned to mixing, the singer didn't feel the same. 'That album's the best we ever did,' he adds. 'Unfortunately, Bill Laswell fucked it up during the mix-down, which is very unfortunate. He let the tapes go to New York and we were all happy about it at first, full of glee. "Wow, this is the best album we've done in years." Then it came back from New York and sounded like shit. I flew to NYC after that to try and save it because I'd gotten no cooperation from Bill, you know, because it was his mix and he wanted it that way. I hadn't taken the rough mixes we'd done home, I trusted Bill Laswell, poor fool me. So I spent three days in New York and then came home pissed off because half of the album isn't even on the album and it really is a different album than the one we made in the studio. I was really pissed off that we'd let ourselves slip with the mix on *Orgasmatron*.

'Bill would be a good producer with anyone else, you know, I was just sick of producers who have their vision of the thing in front of them, ahead of the band's, you know. They don't try to interpret it, they try to put their stamp on it and that was definitely what Bill was doing.'

Like his boss, Pete Gill felt that the mixing wasn't all it

could have been. 'I honestly liked everything on the album,' he admits, 'but my favourite was – you've guessed it – "Orgasmatron". Lemmy, like all of us, had everything down pat before we went in the studios – if you start messing about with the arrangements in the studio it just clouds the issue and costs a lot of money. But some of the overdubs were done while in the studio and that really was where Bill Laswell came in. You know, he would suggest things we hadn't thought of and I must say his production on the track "Orgasmatron" was a masterpiece! We were all extremely happy with the results prior to mixing. Unfortunately, we were far from happy with the final mix – we were contracted to a tour of, I think America, right after recording the album and foolishly agreed to let Bill mix it without us being there. And there were effects and gates on the drums especially that worked superbly on tracks like "Orgasmatron" but took all the power away on the faster tracks like "Riding with the Driver". That was so, so powerful before the final mix but, because of the effects, it made it, in my opinion, so tame. Bill is an amazing producer but I think if we had have been there at the mix it would have been a lot more powerful because I was a really powerful player. Bill loved my playing and asked me to work on some upcoming amazing projects, which I would have done but I didn't have the time, so yes, we were very disappointed. Not really with Bill but because we weren't at the final mix.'

Lemmy expanded on the title of the album in his autobiography. 'I didn't come up with the title *Orgasmatron* right off the bat. The album's working title was *Riding with the Driver*... but that track didn't turn out as good as we'd hoped... I made up the word on my own... A lot of our fans consider the album one of our "classics" and there are some great songs on it – the title track and "Deaf Forever", for example. I'll always have problems with the way it was mixed though. As far as I'm concerned it was only half the album it should have been.'

Fans and critics appeared to disagree, with the former group elevating the album to a UK No. 21 peak on its release on 9 August 1986. The latter – *Billboard* as an example – noted, 'Motörhead appear to be trying something new with *Orgasmatron*, bringing in producer Bill Laswell to put a slightly different slant on their signature sound. Laswell does beef up the mix with added sonic detail, which works to particularly good effect on the title track – the densely layered production helps transform the song and its simple riff into a chugging psychedelic noise-fest.'

Heading back into the studio the very next year, Motörhead would attempt a return to their roots with a stripped-down eighth LP, aptly titled *Rock'n'Roll*. Other changes the band made included dismissing drummer Pete Gill in favour of rehiring Phil 'Philthy' Taylor. 'By June we were back in the studio, recording a new album,' wrote Lemmy in his autobiography, 'which would be *Rock'n'Roll*... [I'd also] given Phil Taylor his job back. It was a mistake in retrospect... but the decision worked all right for a while.'

Drummer Pete Gill recalls the circumstances surrounding his dismissal from the band. "I absolutely loved my time in the band, especially the playing. It was awesome. Lemmy and myself had some bitter disagreements, usually over his selfishness, punctuality and trying to bend the rules – however, on stage it was a match made in heaven and he worked like a Trojan. My motto is, if I am going to push myself to the limits every night, so are you – and he did. I left the band after a very acrimonious fight with Lemmy – I was not, as he said in his rather pathetic book, fired. He also made other derogatory remarks, which again were all untrue. The day I left the band I was so very upset at his attitude when I had given my all twenty-four/seven. I decided enough was enough and decided not to play again. Sad, I know, but something just clicked on that day and my heart told me to walk away from the life I had loved since the age of fifteen. Oh well, happy memories for me and I hope a lot of other people.'

Still, even with familiar drummer Phil Taylor back behind the skins, work on the album did not proceed without the occasional hitch. 'Problems in the studio – nothing truly disastrous – just a series of little annoyances,' elaborates Lemmy. 'Our biggest mistake was choosing Guy Bidmead to produce it. He was an engineer really, so we were pretty much producing it ourselves. Guy had looked like a good idea though. He had worked with Vic Maile, who helped on our two most successful albums... but the chemistry wasn't quite right. It wasn't Guy's fault really – it was us too. We were calling all the shots and whoever was nearest to the desk would generally be the loudest! There was quite a bit of confusion when we were making that album... We didn't have enough time to do the songs properly and when that happens you're pretty much wasting your time.'

Billboard would agree with Lemmy's assessment, highlighting the fact that 'the songwriting here is rather uninspired for the band's standards and the one-two punch of the phenomenal title track and the amusing "Eat the Rich" (the album's only true highlights) are over too soon.' Lemmy, in spite of the general downbeat attitude to the recording, did praise its producer in as much as 'he certainly did a better job of paying attention to what the band wanted to do. He tried to interpret what we wanted on to the album, where Bill Laswell really didn't.' Recalling some of the recording specifics of the album, Lemmy says that 'on *Rock'n'Roll*, I played with a full Marshall stack.' Explaining his writing process for the album's vocal parts, once the band's rhythm tracks had been laid, Lemmy says, 'When I'm adding a song's melody, you can't really play on your own with the bass, so I wrote those to a guitar"

Once principle tracking had wrapped, the band transitioned into mixing. Engineer Arabella Rodriguez: 'We mixed on a fifty-six-channel SSL console, through big JBL monitors. I assisted Guy Bidmead on the mix and

I remember that Lemmy was looking to achieve with the bass sound some of the same thing he did on stage, and we actually had a Groove Tube valve bass amp that had a nine-level output, and we used that on the bass because I remember Guy explained that Lemmy liked his Marshall stack out of phase. So when it came back up into the desk it was out of phase and then Guy would correct it to make it sound proper. I remember that was a moment of amusement, just the way this Groove Tube came into the desk out of phase, that was fun. It was a moment where we tried something as an experiment and it happened to mimic that sound. It was a great session and I remember Guy knew exactly what he was going for. He was very patient and sympathetic, and willing to try new things. Lemmy was around for much of the mixing and he was lovely, a real gentleman. I remember him being happy when the mix was done.'

Released on 15 September 1987, *Rock'n'Roll* peaked at UK No. 34. '*Rock'n'Roll* is a fair album but it isn't one of our best,' admitted Lemmy in his autobiography. 'Even though we've done better records, both before and since, *Rock'n'Roll* did have some great songs, like "Dogs" and "Boogeyman"... Overall, it just didn't seem to work. Still, it's not a bad album – I don't think we've made a bad one.'

Billboard's review appeared to acknowledge something Lemmy had been arguing for years, that being the fact that 'Motörhead are actually a rock'n'roll band in the purest sense. And this release reminds you that, despite their outrageous speed and ear-shattering distortion, Motörhead tunes have much more in common with Chuck Berry than Black Sabbath.' Regrouping after the album's disappointing commercial performance, the band would release another live LP, *No Sleep At All*, before entering the studio in 1990 to record *1916*. It would be an album that was to be better received and would also do well commercially.

Chapter Eight

1916: 1990/1991

Lemmy – bass, vocals
Phil Campbell – guitar
Würzel – guitar
Phil 'Philthy Animal' Taylor – drums
Producer – Peter Solley
Released – 26 February 1991
Peak Chart Position: UK No. 24

Motörhead entered Sunset Sound Studios in late 1990 to record their first album of the new decade and ninth studio LP overall. Lemmy recalled in his autobiography, 'We were working on a new record… Of course, being Motörhead, it couldn't possibly go off without a hitch. The first thing we had to overcome was the album's original producer, Ed Stasium. We recorded four songs with him before we decided he had to go… After that, we got Pete Solley, who was great.'

Solley found it an attractive offer. 'I think it piqued my curiosity to work with Motörhead,' says the producer. 'I've always been drawn to guitar bands, going back to the romantics. I'd worked with Mountain and, in fact, Lemmy heard of me through Mountain. He heard the Mountain record I did and liked the guitar sounds on that, so that's what drew him to me. It was really something out of my comfort zone too because I'd never done a metal record, just a hardcore record, a Motörhead record before.'

Of the characteristically tight schedule, the producer says that they 'just showed up and went straight into pre-production. We did about ten days of pre-production, that's what I normally do, ten days and up to two weeks, depending on the artist, in a rehearsal room. And we worked on the musical side – rather than the lyrical side – at that point, working with the drums, particularly with the bass, getting that right. So when you get into the studio, your foundation is good, just making sure the bottom-end parts are right, making sure that we understand the parameters of the song, the rhythms.

The way I work, I think it's very important to over-rehearse, so when you get in the studio, it comes easily. That's my attitude and I think Motörhead were very good in that regard, if I recall right. They were extremely well behaved and extremely dedicated, and I think they worked very hard. Not as long, maybe, as other bands I've worked with but then it's more high pressure and hardcore than other bands, so you can't really rehearse for eight hours or you'd all be absolutely exhausted. Of course, with Lemmy, that wasn't really a problem – I was just amazed he was still alive in general when I met him, that has always amazed me. It's even more amazing he's still alive today.'

In the course of shaping the songs for the band's new album, Lemmy explained in his autobiography that 'several of the songs on *1916* – "Love Me Forever" and "1916", for example – were very different from anything we'd done before, but it's not like we were trying to change; we just did. What surprised people (in a positive manner, I hasten to add) were some of the other tracks. "Nightmare/The Dreamtime" and "1916" both relied heavily on keyboards, which was very different for Motörhead – or any heavy band in 1990. In fact, *1916* also had cello and no guitars whatsoever.'

Peter Solley was pleased by the response of the band to being taken in new musical directions. Lemmy was, he remembers, very open. 'I think he was surprisingly open to suggestions and I think we got on very well. I think that's everything because he's a difficult son of a bitch and he hadn't got on with most of the people he'd worked with, but we got on. We seemed to really hit it off and, even though we would argue viciously for the entire process of both albums I did, we both came to the best conclusion, I think, so that was good. He was like a sparring partner; that's how he treated me.'

At the same time, Lemmy didn't break with Motörhead's

norms in terms of production. 'Quite a lot of *1916* is exactly what our fans had come to expect from us, only better, of course,' the singer wrote in his autobiography. 'Take "I'm So Bad" – it's a loud rock'n'roll song with absurd lyrics, just typical Motörhead... Then there's my usual Chuck Berry fixation in "Going to Brazil". "R.A.M.O.N.E.S", the fastest and shortest song on the album, actually started off as a slow number. Then at one point I said, "Let's play it a bit faster," and it sounded just like the Ramones, so that's how that came about. And although "Angel City" was just about living [in Los Angeles], I wrote the lyrics before I moved... It was one of them songs where I cracked myself up writing it. I was all by myself, laughing outrageously. And we put some saxophone on it – that was something new.'

The band swiftly got on with the business of getting the tracks down. 'We recorded the album at Sunset Sound,' says Solley, 'and I remember they had a nice Neve console we were working on and a nice live room. The band tracked live off the floor together and, for the drum miking, I used close mics, room mics – some Neumanns, maybe four Neumanns in different parts of the room to get a nice slap-back, basic overheads, nothing fancy, 451s or 87s, various Schoep microphones. On the kick drum, we used a 421 with a D12.'

The legendary sound of the band's bass prompted a dry comment from the producer. 'Lemmy, of course, his sound is completely unique – I'd never worked with anyone who played the bass in that manner. He doesn't have any bottom end, he uses a guitar amp as his amplifier and then he has these four stacks — and half of them have speakers blown in them but that was part of his sound, this kind of crunch, so I think we spent a long time on Lemmy, working up the sound because it's a very difficult sound to record. No bottom end — it's all mid-range and a lot of overtones and its difficult because, as I say, you can't go in and put your ear anywhere near the amp, because you'll get blasted. So I probably took a whole day getting that.'

Continuing, he recalls, 'Motörhead is the old "my amps go up to eleven" so everything's flat out. And it's hard getting a guitar sound or a bass sound with a band like that because you can't go in the studio and listen — because you would go deaf.

'So there was heavy isolation and my usual set-up would be a close mic on the amp, which would be a Shure 57 or a 421, a simple mic, then experiment with some ambient miking and that's a trial-and-error process; there's no definitive method. In pre-production, you get rid of the solos because in the studio they're overdubbed. So we worked with the guitar parts. The guitars were pretty straight ahead, the Marshall stacks, each one was isolated. I didn't go in with any preconceived plan about amplification or mics or anything like that, it's just a question of hearing it — you get an idea, you put the close mic on and put the mic about three or four feet away and have a listen and say, "Mmmm, let's try the next speaker, its pretty good, let's try the next." You work your way around and it's a process of elimination, finding the best speaker and then processing with some compression, and put it through a pulsic or some [other] kind of tube equalisation. But I don't think the guitars were any problem. I think the bass took a real long time.'

Offering fans insight into the band's song development process in the studio, Solley begins by explaining, 'Back then they had two guitar players with Würzel and Phil Campbell but Lemmy was definitely the musical director – so to speak – of the band. Phil was involved to a larger degree and Phil Taylor, the drummer, we got rid of him by the second record. Würzel was probably more passive than Phil, so it was really Phil and Lemmy who were the driving forces. Phil's a very good guitar player and quite creative, so I'd say those were the two who were in charge.'

In an interview with *Rolling Stone*, Lemmy insisted that the defining sound of the band has remained largely unchanged throughout its various incarnations. 'The central axis is the music that we originally started out doing with Eddie and Phil in the band. They've gone but the basic idea is the same because it was my idea and I'm still here. And other people come in and contribute their styles and we try some experimental stuff like [on] *1916*.'

That experimentation, as Lemmy elaborated on in an interview with *Chart* magazine, evolved, in part, out of his refusal to be pigeon-holed. Even when there were those who believed his band shouldn't stray from their signature sound at all. 'Fuck 'em!' he said. 'I ain't playing for those people. See, they wanna keep me in a box that they made. It's not my box and I ain't gonna get in it. I'll play what the fuck I want. I was raised on early rock'n'roll and The Beatles, where you did anything you liked. Every time a Beatles LP came out, it was like a different band. You had to really work on liking it and it was worth it too because you found different things in there. I don't want to be obvious.'

In that spirit, Lemmy was as adventurous as ever with his lyric writing on *1916*. Of the title track, he revealed in his autobiography, 'I wrote the words before I wrote the music. It's about the Battle of the Somme in WWI… When it [the track] happened, I was in England, watching a programme about WWI, and I had a brainstorm when they got to the Battle of the Somme.' Lemmy wasn't daunted by using historical sources and other outside influences in his lyrics. 'Lyrics and poetry are a lot alike,' he told the band's website. 'Quite a bit of my lyrics could stand on their own as poetry. Especially songs like "1916"… stuff like that.'

'Nightmare/The Dreamtime' were among the more controversial lyrics on the album. They set Lemmy on a collision course with the likes of Tipper Gore, wife of former Vice President Al Gore and co-founder of the Parents Music Resource Center, the organisation which campaigns against explicit words in songs. The song, Lemmy told his band's website, was all about him saying, 'You bastards are never gonna tell me what I can fucking sing about.'

Peter Solley was full of admiration for the words that Lemmy came out with for his songs. 'He's a great lyricist, Lemmy, I have to give him his due. We would go through the lyrics but that's the easiest part with Lemmy, I think. He's really an excellent lyricist, so there really was not a lot to do and he usually came into the studio where he would pretty well have it done.'

The singer and his producer began laying down the vocals. Solley recalled, 'We recorded on a Neumann 87. What we'd normally do is put up four different mics and have the singer try each one, and whichever one sounded best, we went with – and we ended up with an 87 on that record. All of Lemmy's vocals were three takes – we were well-rehearsed or else we would work it out that night, so they really had it down, then come back in the next day and be able to put it down quickly. That was the general approach. He would do maybe two vocal takes for each lead vocal, that's all his headphones would take too because they were so loud – they would blow up. You'd have to keep replacing the headphones. I remember the tech department at the studio kept having to repair them all day because they were so loud that [it] was a problem on the mic. He had them louder than anyone I've ever known, louder than you would think was humanly possible. I'd say to him, "Lemmy, you're going to be so deaf in a year or two," and he'd say, "Well, I've gotten this far." If you stood three feet [away] with the track going, it was deafening, coming out of the headphones, just unbelievable. So I remember that was a problem with the vocals because, as soon as he'd start singing, the racket from the headphones would come crashing in and I think we had to gate it if I recall, it was so loud. I used effects on his vocals

– nothing extravagant, some reverb, it was a very organic process. Not a lot of tricks; both on *1916* and *March ör Die*, it was pretty straight ahead.'

As principle recording wrapped, Lemmy and his band 'were quite happy', he recalled in his autobiography. It was time to get on with mixing. Solley recalled that 'on the first album, *1916*, I had the guitars way up in the front of the mix. Where Lemmy's bass was concerned, it was odd because he plays with his sound the way it is and yet, when we did it, after we'd listen to it, he'd say, "There's no bass on the record." And I'd say, "Well, Lemmy, that's because you have no bass on your amp. You're playing a bass but you're playing it through a guitar amp." Plus, he used a Rickenbacker bass, which tends not to have any bass either. So when we came to mix it, we put on as much bass as we could in equalisation but then he would come back to me and say, "Well, I played it at the Whiskey next to another record and there's no bass on it." And I would say, "Well, Lemmy, that's the sound of Motörhead, there's no bass per se." If you go and see them live, there's not a lot of bass. So that was always an ongoing debate. He didn't get defensive, he was all right with it but he just wanted more.'

Released on 16 February 1991, *1916* reached UK No. 16, marking something of a comeback for the band, following the under-performance of their last studio LP. *Billboard* later hailed the album as one that showed the band hadn't 'changed much and time hadn't made its sledgehammer approach any less appealing… Motörhead is as inspired as ever on *1916*,' while *Rolling Stone* concluded, '*1916* reapplies [the band's] sonic grit with a trowel… The sound remains the same, dependably raw and uncompromising across the decades.' Perhaps the most unexpected praise the band received for the album – and more broadly an acknowledgement of their longevity – came in the form of a Grammy award nomination for Best Metal Performance.

Lemmy commented to hardradio.com that even winning wouldn't have made any difference to them. 'It wouldn't have lasted,' he declared. 'We don't play the game. I had a great speech ready in the event we had won. I was going to say, "I'm not going to thank anybody. None of you fuckers have ever given us a hand. You didn't do anything. We did it all by ourselves. Thank you very much. Good night."'

Producer Peter Solley, for his own part, considered the nomination to be a truly proud moment in his career. 'When we got nominated for a Grammy with *1916*, which I thought was brilliant and didn't see that coming, it was quite a thrill, actually,' he recalls. 'I've made quite a lot of records and had never gotten a Grammy nomination. So that nomination certificate is on my wall with my gold records.' Ironically, Motörhead lost out to their stylistic offspring Metallica. Still, heading into 1992 and their next album, the band appeared commercially rejuvenated and ready with their next studio outing to *March ör Die*.

Chapter Nine

March ör Die: 1992

Lemmy – bass, lead vocals, cello arrangements

Phil Campbell (billed as Zööm) – guitar

Würzel – guitar

Tommy Aldridge – drums

Phil 'Philthy Animal' Taylor – drums on 'I Ain't No Nice Guy'

Mikkey Dee – drums on 'Hellraiser'

Producer – Peter Solley

Released – 14 August 1992

Hot off the heels of 1991's album *1916*, the band entered Music Grinder Studios in Los Angeles in early 1992 to record their second LP for Sony with Peter Solley. The major challenge the producer faced with the album was navigating tracking with long-time drummer Phil Taylor. 'When we started on *March ör Die*,' says Solley, 'Phil was still the drummer. He was the drummer during rehearsals and was the drummer when we started recording, and we recorded about ten days of tracks and I was very unhappy with the drums – I thought the timing and sound weren't great. So I started suggesting the possibility of our bringing another drummer in and, at that point, I think Lemmy was kind of all for it.'

Guitarist Phil Campbell seemed to be in agreement too. 'Philthy came back after Peter Gill left and… when he rejoined the band he was a little bit ropey,' said Campbell in an interview with Big Shout/Rock'n'Roll Experience/K2K.com, 'We thought he was away for three years or so and that he'd be better but, unfortunately, he couldn't cut it… the first two CDs, his drumming was pretty good and we thought, oh, we could just get back into it now and we'll be back up to top form. But he just kept going down and down. It was a shame. He's a nice guy but he just couldn't manage it in the end… We gave him a couple of years to get better. It was something we thought really hard about because he is a very nice guy. He's a lunatic but a nice guy. But if you can't manage to drum for a band, you just can't do it… I loved the guy to death but he could only do the one straight drum beat and it's a shame.'

Lemmy's own disappointment with Taylor's drumming performances had been building for several years. 'Philthy was never as good when he came back,' he said in 1995. 'He was great before he left… He had to come back because his band that was going to be so much better than Motörhead failed miserably. So I gave him his gig back and I don't think he ever forgave me for giving it to him… [After that,] he got worse, not better. When he first got back, he wasn't that bad; then he went… well, by the end, it was like, "What the fuck was that?"… His excuse was, "Oh, I was improvising," and he couldn't remember any of the new songs.'

In the same interview, Campbell recalled that 'in LA, two days before we do the recording for the new album, he breaks his Walkman. We'd go into rehearsals and they were crap and I'd say, "Philthy, you don't know any of the fucking songs, man." And he'd say, "Well, the thing is, my Walkman's broke."… It was getting bad. He couldn't play four bars without fucking up. For three years when he rejoined, we gave it our best shot but… he couldn't see anything wrong with his drumming, which was even worse… He just didn't have it for some reason… If he would say, "I know where I fucked up," that's one thing but what he didn't realise was that he was a major fuck-up. We'd be in the studio practicing and he'd be out washing his car.'

Once the decision had been made to replace Taylor, Lemmy was tasked – in his capacity as band leader – with giving the drummer the news. Solley: 'I think he'd been thinking about it, so what we did – and it was very hard because he had to tell Phil that was it – was we brought in Ozzy Osbourne's drummer Tommy Aldridge, who is not credited on the record and he didn't want to be credited. And he came in and we re-did the drums on most of the tracks. He's the loudest drummer I've ever worked with, he just defined the parts, he was unbelievably good. It was like another band when he started playing — it was huge, the difference. The power, the assertiveness, he played great. He played so hard and so loud that literally he'd be in the middle of doing these takes and his drums would fall apart! I mean, drums would fall off the set because he was hitting them so hard, it was astounding. I believe he's on the full album, even though he never got a credit. I don't think anyone could have done it better, he was just perfect.'

Recording got back underway with Tommy Aldridge in the drummer's chair. 'By the time 1992 had begun, we were working on songs for the next Motörhead record, which came to be known as *March ör Die*,' wrote Lemmy in his autobiography. 'We used Pete Solley again but — as often happens with our producers — he wasn't as good the second time around.' The producer took a contrasting view to the latter, particularly when it came to recording Lemmy's bass guitar — though he does remember there were differences of opinion. 'On most of the *March ör Die* record,' says Solley, 'I actually… would double his bass with a synthesizer, very quietly, a bottom-end synth. I doubled him on the bottom and you can't really even hear it, it's almost subsonic. And it really gave it a lot more bottom end, so it would sound more in keeping with other records. I don't know if it was a good idea or a bad idea — it might have been better to keep it as it was — because they were the only band in the world that had that kind of sound. But that was always a fighting issue — bass bottom end.'

There were, however, other areas of the album's production

where keys showed up without objection from the band, the producer explaining, 'We were trying to broaden their approach and trying to add to the basic Motörhead colours – which is the flat-out crunch – and looking to add colour where there weren't before, changing things up so it wasn't about doing a guitar here but, instead, doing a piano here. It went over very well with the band. We definitely all thought it was the right thing. The piano on the record was all played live.'

Lemmy contacted metal superstar peers to make guest appearances on the album, among them Guns N' Roses' lead guitarist Slash, who played guitar on 'You Better Run' and the lead solo on 'I Ain't No Nice Guy' alongside Ozzy Osbourne. He shared lead vocals with Lemmy on the single 'Hellraiser'.

Solley found recording Slash's guitar parts to be 'interesting because, whenever someone is a big star, for whatever they do – guitars, vocals – they're usually very good and Slash was very good. He came in, sat in the control room and had a Marshall stack, which he brought and he plugged directly into the amp with no effects and just got a great sound. That's really the test of a great guitar player, if they can just plug into the amp and get that great big fat sound because it all comes from the hands and the actual instrument. And he was one of those who could do that. He did between forty minutes and an hour of recording, so we'd do a part, then do another track, bounce them around. He was drinking and was still very good.'

Of the techniques employed by Black Sabbath's front man, the producer recalls, 'Ozzy doubles his vocal when he records. So you do the first track and it's just one take and you think, eh, that's pretty good, I don't know. And then he says, "Let's double it," so you go straight into doubling it and immediately you hear Ozzy. It's amazing. He has his own thing and he always doubles – you can't always tell because he doubles very closely – but when that double goes on, that's when you hear Ozzy. It's that instantly identifiable sound, so recording him was easy as pie, could not have been easier. One of the easiest things I've ever done was recording Ozzy. He used the same mic as Lemmy.'

In another departure from the procedure the band were used to, Lemmy recalled, in his biography, 'The record company wanted us to cover a standard. We came up with the idea of doing Ted Nugent's "Cat Scratch Fever". Frankly, I like our version of it better than Ted's... I suggested it and they were kind of, "I don't know," and I said, "We could do a great version of this, you can Motörhead it and it could be successful, it could be one of those tracks."

'But that was the track that probably least appealed to them and I thought it was a great idea, and Lemmy wasn't sure – maybe he was right – I'm not sure. I thought it might be a single and I still don't think it was a bad move to do it but I guarantee the band never played it live. Sometimes that kind of thing works, sometimes it doesn't, you have to try things. I think it worked but maybe it wasn't right for Motörhead. My hat is off to Lemmy for being willing to try it and it says something about our relationship that he even thought about it.'

For all the sonic experimentation, Solley felt that the sessions had gone well. 'When we finished that second record, I felt pretty damn good, actually,' he confirms. 'I felt Lemmy and I got on very well, once you understand him – and like I said, Lemmy is difficult – and accept him for who he is, that his breakfast is a Bourbon and Scotch and you accept it, he's great to work with. Together, I felt we had taken a step forward that they had never taken before and really had achieved what we'd set out to do, which was open it all up a bit and try to get a little more commercial – although I realise that's a terrible word. But when we played the album back, I thought they really sounded like they had a musicality that hadn't been there before. Before it was an organic, orgasmic experience, which was brilliant, but now we'd added a different facet. There was still some of that on the record but there was also a side that showed thoughtfulness and a side that showed a minimalist approach to some of it. To where there was a little thought involved: do we really need this? Do we really want that? So I thought it was real successful and the album sounded really good in the studio.'

Heading into mixing, the producer explains, 'I think we kept a lot of what we did on the first record re: the approach, but we worked on the bass – that was a big different thing, of course – and we worked on maybe inching down the guitars a hair so they weren't quite as spiky as on *1916*, making the vocals more of a statement as opposed to the vocals being, as they had been up to that point, sort of in the track – sitting in behind the guitars almost. This time I think we made them more up front, which was a departure. We took more time too, mixing. I think [with] the whole record we spent more money than [on] *1916*, so we took it and mixed it at SoundCastle, which is in Hollywood. It's an SSL room where they do a lot of film work and was brilliant.

I remember the last song on *March ör Die* was the "1916" of that album; it was a collage of sounds and effects, and that was a bitch – I remember we worked on that for days. Lemmy had a vision of how it would sound and it never quite sounded as he wanted it to sound but we did our best.' Lemmy elaborated in his autobiography on the difficulties of recording it. 'The title track to the album was the sticking point 'cause he had his version of "March ör Die" and that was it. I wanted a few things changed and he didn't help me at all. He just sat there, put his feet up on a chair and let the engineer work on it. I thought that was a bit crappy. That's why "March ör Die" didn't work. It should have: it was a tremendous track and I have a couple of takes of it on tape that are much better than the version on the album.'

The producer turned his attention to mixing the album's drum tracks. 'It became obvious when we were mixing that Tommy Aldridge would have been the perfect drummer for them,' believes Solley, 'and I felt he definitely brought new life to the record and rounded out the broader sound I was going for on *March ör Die* because he defined the parts. As opposed to where before you didn't really notice Phil's deficiencies because it was so guitar friendly, that all you really heard was the snare drum and the kick, and that was it. Once we started doing stuff that wasn't as obviously guitar heavy, you started to notice the deficiency in the drums that had been hidden up to that point. So once we realised "wow, the drums aren't taking up the space they need to be in the right ways", it became a unanimous thing getting another drummer in. So Mikkey Dee came in after we finished the record.'

Mikkey Dee had played with both Don Dokken and King Diamond. In an interview with *Drum God* magazine, he confirmed *March ör Die* 'was finished when I joined the band. They wanted me to re-do the whole album but Peter – he was the producer – they didn't have the budget to start doing drums again. It was almost finished… He did a good job for the time he did it in. He was called in and did it in two days – *bam, bam, bam* – and I don't like those drums at all. I think Tommy Aldridge is a very square drummer. That's his style, he's very square. And I'm, myself, a lot rounder. I adore drummers like Ian Paice, Brian Downey, who have a round feel to it. And Tommy's very square… To replace Philthy Animal on drums was nothing hard – playing-wise – but, you know, he is a character and he's been playing with Motörhead for ever, so that could be a problem because, if you talk to a lot of loyal fans, they don't care how bad he was, they just want to see Taylor... He's Motörhead all the way through his bones, you know. In the old days it was great, he was a good drummer, but some musicians are like that, they have to practice every day only to be average. I think he is one of them. Then Pete Gill, technically a lot better drummer, but no fucking charisma whatsoever. He didn't fit in the band at all, I'd say, and he was never accepted by the Motörhead fans either for some reason, I don't know why. But Taylor, a super character, a fun guy, Motörhead all the way through, maybe more problems with his drumming but Pete Gill, better technically but absolutely more or less the same character as the flower over there – you know what I mean?'

Lemmy was very enthusiastic about the arrival of his new band member. 'Mikkey Dee, in a way, saved us because he is the best drummer that we've ever had. He's excellent,' he told *Moo* magazine. And in his autobiography he continued in the same vein, explaining how Mikkey came into his orbit. 'I'd known Mikkey for many years. Motörhead did a tour with Mercyful Fate when Brian Robertson was in our band and Mikkey was their drummer. In fact, I'd asked him to join the band once before, around the time Pete Gill joined up, but he was just joining Dokken at the time so he couldn't do it. This time, I cornered him at the Rainbow – he was living in LA at the time – and he was free. So we tried him out. The first thing Mikkey did with us was "Hellraiser" and he was very good immediately. It was obvious that it was going to work... We did two songs with him in the studio… and then we immediately went out on the road with Ozzy.'

Being in Don Dokken had seemed like a good idea at the time, Dee told rockezine.com journalist Roger Lotring. But he came to understand that it just couldn't last. 'I joined Don 'cause that's exactly what I wanted to do – go more commercial and just sit down and do just a regular rock beat,' declared the drummer. 'And that was the best college I went through. We had a great time over the years I played with Don and it was fantastic. I grew so much as a drummer… [Then] I just realised I'm not a pop drummer, I [had] to join a real heavy band again… Motörhead was perfect when I left Don – Lemmy called me two weeks later and that's when we got going.

'I was used to doing all kinds of difficult patterns and other technical stuff when I was with King Diamond, while Lemmy just wanted me to lay down a straightforward rock'n'roll beat. This was very hard for me in the beginning, I'll tell you that… Ever since 1986, Lemmy must have asked me to join his band more than five times. When I finally said "yes" I wanted to put something from my technical skills into the Motörhead sound… [but ultimately], I'm a rock drummer. I'm a heavy drummer.'

Motörhead might have thought they had experienced enough chaos during the album's recording and afterwards with the arrival of their new drummer. But that wasn't all. 'Quite a bit went on during that time in addition to our changing drummers,' revealed Lemmy in his autobiography.

Motörhead In the Studio

'For one thing, Los Angeles had a riot after the Rodney King verdict. We were at the Music Grinder [studio], which was in the east part of Hollywood – right on Hollywood Boulevard, in fact – recording "Hellraiser", rather appropriately. I came out from doing my vocal and there was a TV in the lounge showing a burning house. And I looked outside a window and saw the very same house from the other side! It was right down the street! Everything was on fire, people were running around – it was complete mayhem. Mikkey was there and he was screaming, "My car! My car's outside!" and the guy from the studio came in and said, "We've got to cut it a bit short today, boys."'

Peter Solley: 'During the mixing, they had the LA riots. I remember driving home and seeing the National Guard out on Hollywood Boulevard and I remember we had to have a guard in front of the studio because everything was being trashed.'

But the band survived unscathed and the album proved to be wellreceived by the critics. '*March ör Die* easily confiscates Ted Nugent's "Cat Scratch Fever" as another Lemmy anthem,' said *Rolling Stone*, while *Billboard* took the opportunity to celebrate the group as 'arguably the most important underground band in rock history'. Lemmy seemed particularly pleased with a review which praised the song 'I'm So Bad Baby (I Don't Care)', explaining in an interview with roughedge.com, 'I have a great time playing this one. It's also one of the funniest lyrics I've ever written. Just to show you how humorous the radical feminist ranks

128

can get – some woman at *Melody Maker* called this song sexist when it came out!'

Lemmy felt his label was far less well-disposed to the band than the critics had been. In interviews with aural-innovations.com and a fansite he claimed the band 'had a hit record on the radio with "I Ain't No Nice Guy…" from *March ör Die* with Ozzy and Slash on it and they actually killed it on purpose because it wasn't their idea. I said to them, "Get it on the AOR playlist, cross it over," and they said, "We tried this and we tried that, it's dead," and I said, "You're a fucking liar, you got no fucking time to push it. Forget it, we'll do it." So we got our own people to push it. We got the song and album on the radio, and it was high on the playlist, so we went to the label and said, "We got your artist Ozzy on this tune and Slash. Let's make a video for the song," and they [Sony/Epic] said "no"! So we made our own video – it wasn't great but it was all right.

'We took it to MTV and they never played it, and it went dead on the radio… Talk about cutting off your nose to spite your face. One guy from Sony/Epic actually called up some DJ in Kansas City and said, "Don't play this, we didn't give it to you!" They were fucking the worst. They were the pits. We got a Grammy for our first record for them and we were supposed to be a spent force who they were picking up out of the kindness of their hearts. We got nominated for this Grammy and, when I went along to the ceremonies, the guy from Sony never even came out to say hello to me. Because we are Motörhead… too bad for him.'

Lemmy clearly felt that the album was a lost opportunity. 'Overall,' he wrote in his autobiography, *March ör Die* is underrated.' For his part, producer Peter Solley felt, looking back over his two-album collaboration with Motörhead, that with both *1916* and *March ör Die*, 'we made two brilliant albums'.

Chapter Ten

Bastards: 1993

Lemmy – bass, vocals
Phil Campbell – guitar
Würzel – guitar
Mikkey Dee – drums
Producing, mixing and digital editing – Howard Benson
Engineering and mixing – Ryan Dorn
Released – 29 November 1993

In 1992 Motörhead hooked up with a new producer, Howard Benson, to record their 11th studio LP, *Bastards*. 'For the better part of our careers, it seemed like Motörhead changed producers every other album,' said Lemmy in his autobiography. 'Jimmy Miller did two, as did Vic Maile and Peter Solley. They never seemed to be any good for more than that. I think we wear them out! I don't remember the name of the other guy we were looking at for the new record but it was between him and Howard Benson, and we went with Howard. Howard certainly earned the gig: he was keen and he came to all the rehearsals (though I have to say it was the last time he did that!). Howard was there, Howard was gonna do this record whatever fucking happened. He just came and hung around until we said "yes". That's really what he did – in the end, we just said, "Fuck it! Let's let him do it!"'

Benson, for his own part, recalls, 'Todd Singerman, Motörhead's manager, had heard about me through another band I produced called Bang Tango and Lemmy liked how that record sounded, so when they approached me about doing Motörhead, I said, "I'll give it a shot".'

Engineer Ryan Dorn: 'We got the call out of the blue. We were working at Sunset Studios on Cherokee, on a band called Seed, and Howard hung up the phone and said, "Oh my God, we just got a shot at meeting Lemmy and doing the next Motörhead record." And to be honest, I knew "Ace of Spades" and a couple other songs but was in no sense of the words a Motörhead aficionado. But we took the meeting and Lemmy was the most animated human that I think I'd ever met. He came in to Sunset and Lemmy always rolls without any sort of pomp and circumstance; what you see is what you get with that guy. There's no qualms about it, that is not a stage persona, that is who he is: he is rock'n'roll standing on two legs, the epitome of heavy rock'n'roll. There's no doubt he's the father of it – I think he invented it. And so when he came in there was no need to sell the band or sell the project or idea. When we met with him – and we knew he was going to be a handful just because he was so animated and opinionated, because he is a veteran of the business – I think he said, "I want to make a fucking great record, mate," so we slated a start date three or four months in the future. When Howard and I finished the record we'd been working on, we rolled up our sleeves and went into pre-production on *Bastards*. Motörhead rehearsed for at least a couple weeks in pre-production, five or six days a week, eight hours a day.'

Benson explains, 'I was very involved with the arrangements of the songs and the vocal parts, so I was basically the musical guy. As a producer, that's what I do to this day.' Engineer Ryan Dorn recalls that he 'first hooked up with Howard because we'd both worked with TSOL [punk band True Sound of Liberty] and we became a producer–engineer team – this was through the early 1990s. We worked well together because Howard had a lot of great ideas with regard to the recording process as a producer while I was very focused on the art of recording and getting performances out of people. Howard was more of an arranger. Prior to Motörhead, we worked on a Bang Tango album and some other records.'

Lemmy detailed the band's songwriting process in an interview with the *Columbus Dispatch*. 'It's always pretty much under the knife,' he told them. 'We always wrote like that. It suits us. When Mikkey joined us, he couldn't believe it. He was horrified. He said, "You cannot work like this!" I said, "Yeah, you can. Look.'"

For Ryan Dorn it was like the start of any new relationship. 'When you're first working with somebody, you've got something to prove and that is a two-side-of-the-glass kind of thing,' he says. 'The artist wants to show the new team how badass they are and, conversely, the producer and the engineer want to do the absolute best that they can for the artist. So it's like a first date, where everyone wants to do the best they can. So Lemmy came to the table with some really really great songs – "Born to Raise Hell", which if they had a shot at radio, that was the one; also "On Your Feet or On Your Knees", which was absolutely relentless, etc. – that in pre-production really stood out as just rock'n'roll, anthemic, grade-A Motörhead.

'And when you hear songs like that, what I think happens, although I don't think it's an intentional thing, [is that] that song becomes your darling, and you do focus extra energy and perhaps take a little bit more time intrinsically knowing that "hey, this could be the one that really generates some interest and does good for the band". That's not to say you're falling asleep at the console and chewing gum on the other songs but you're very careful as these songs begin to take on a life of their own and to unfold that you're really doing the utmost justice to that particular song. "Born to Raise Hell" had a very identifiable and simple lyric, wasn't too self-indulgent, was very relatable, great chords, a typical Motörhead hit.'

Bastards: 1993

Producer Howard Benson offers his own insight into how working with Lemmy was different from other collaborations 'because, first of all, you don't really get a lot of say in it because it's his thing. I get a lot more say on that stuff with my other artists because that's just the way it goes. It's kind of like because I do a lot of pop-rock stuff, we have to rewrite and rewrite and rewrite – with Lemmy you don't rewrite. It is what it is. I told him if I didn't like something and he would rewrite it but some of the songs, that's just the way it is.'

One party whose input Lemmy seemed to welcome into the process was the drummer. 'This was the first time Mikkey was in with us from the start and he turned out to be even better than we expected,' Lemmy said in his autobiography. 'Phil Taylor hadn't been interested in the writing process for a very long time before we fired him… [But Mikkey] was very involved in the songwriting process for this album.'

Howard Benson dived headlong into developing the arrangements for the songs the band was coming up with in pre-production. 'My first experience with Lemmy almost put me in the hospital because… let's put it this way… he's a really great guy and I love him to death but he's really hard to work with sometimes. Not in a bad way but because he's a purist and is very pure at what he does so, in some ways, you have to kind of accept that as part of what you do with him. I went in there with one set of ears and he went in there with another set of ears, and I wanted

127

his stuff to be more commercial with real songs put together right and all that. And he wanted to do what he usually does, which is the way he does it. And I brought my kind of arrangement sensibilities to the party and, at first, he didn't like it. They were doing everything they could to intimidate me, he and Phil, and in some ways it was good fun but in other ways it was really, really tough to do... really hard.'

For Ryan Dorn, the opportunity to work in A&M Studios was the stuff of dreams. It meant he could 'cut rhythm tracks on the Neve console — as an engineer, that's like going to the Ferrari dealership and getting to test drive an Enzo. More hit, great-sounding records had been done in that room than in a lot of other studios. I've never been a big track-on-an-SSL-console guy, even though I learned on an SSL, mixed on an SSL – those old Neves with the class-A design, that's the shit, hands down. If you fuck up making a great-sounding record at A&M, you should pretty much go sell shoes in my opinion.'

The band settled into recording and their producer got to see their unique way of doing things at first hand. 'On *Bastards* I had the band track live off the floor together,' he revealed, 'but we went back and re-recorded everything over again. Mikkey Dee, half the time, didn't even want anyone in his headphones; he would just do it himself. So once they got the arrangements together, he didn't want to hear anybody. He would say, "OK, I'm ready to go," and we'd hit record and he'd play to a click track, and that was it because he knew what parts he wanted. He was a really great drummer and he was a big upgrade for them, I think.'

It was Dorn who set up the sound for the drummer. 'When I was miking up Mikkey Dee's kit with the two kick drums,' he says, 'I'd actually bumped into Shelly Atkis, who I was a big fan of as the technical guy at A&M and, originally, I'd wanted to use a D112, and [Shelly] said, "Dude, you have to try our D12s," which are the older AKGs… Up until that point, I had never tried the mic and he was right, they were incredible. So we had D12s on the inside of the kicks, Fet47s on the outside, 57s top and bottom on the snare, either a KM84 or 451 on the high-hat, 421s on the toms and U67s on the overheads.' Lemmy recalled the drummer's performances in his autobiography. 'Mikkey also came through when we got in the studio. He banged out the drum tracks in record time. He was amazing and has continued to be amazing to this day.'

The front man took his own turn in the studio and Howard Benson remembers, 'Lemmy was definitely the loudest bass player I've ever recorded. It was ridiculously loud, so much so that we used to wear airplane earmuffs in the studio. That's how loud it got — you're talking about 160 dB and you could get ear damage recording him. His amps were called Killer and Murder — those were the names he gave his two bass amps. In fact, the distorted bass tone I use on all my records now I got from him, actually; I really liked the sound he got. I liked the way it sounded and the way it felt, so I started using a general semblance of that sound on a lot of albums.'

'It isn't rocket science with these guys,' joked Dorn. 'It's all about capturing the performance.' Lemmy echoed the latter in his autobiography, revealing, 'When [Mikkey] first began recording with us he was surprised at the way we do everything off the cuff. He was used to people like Don Dokken who work on the same record for three years and have everything planned out beforehand. I can't stand working that way. We go in with nothing and just hammer it out. It costs less that way and, obviously, it works. If it didn't, we'd do it another way.' And the hammering didn't always go smoothly. 'In the studio, those guys had a lot of arguments within the band,' recalls Benson. 'They went so far back in time that they would argue about things that happened like twenty years ago and I had no idea where the arguments were coming from. And there's some of that that's very charming because it just shows their history and longevity, and how long they've been doing it.'

The producer tried, like many before him, to take the band in some new musical directions. He was more successful than most. 'I didn't really know enough about their stuff at that point,' acknowledges Benson. 'I'd listened to some of their music but all I knew is that I wanted to make a big hit rock record with them and that was it, and I just think Lemmy trusted me enough after a certain point that he let me do what I wanted to do. That's why we ended up working so long together... I think we both realised we were good for each other: he was good for me, I was good for him. So a lot of the elements — like the B3 Hammond, keyboards, etc. — was stuff that he secretly did like to do but really maybe never had someone do it. So when I started doing the acoustic stuff, I remember him saying how much he liked it and we kind of just stuck with it.'

Guitarist Phil Campbell detailed his guitar set-up for the recording in an interview with www.k2k.com. 'My main one is a LAG Explorer, it's a French company. I use a Claymore custom, Kramer guitars, Gallien-Krueger amplifiers, Marshall amplifiers. Depends on what I want to use. I have nineteen stacks all together.'

Ryan Dorn notes that the band would 'have five cabinets going but I would always wind up only using one or two mics and a room mic. It's not like every cabinet was miked. Certainly, you've got the impact of all those multiple drivers firing off in the room from the room mic but I would basically pick the best-sounding tone. Keep in mind these were not the state-of-the-art, rented cabinets from Andy Brauer, these were either loaned to us or were Motörhead's touring stuff. So some of the speakers were blown, some had better mid-range response, others were bright. So I would pretty much pick the actual tones that sounded the best and would make the recording the best.

'A&M Studios — half of the charm and the reason that that Neve room sounded so good is that they had remote mic-pre's and — this is a little-known secret I'll let out of the bag — they actually had remote mic-pre's that you would roll on carts, up to the drums. So you would use the shortest mic-cable length to get to the mic-pre, then they would drive the signal into the desk at line level, so the long run is at a line level versus a mic level. In my opinion, that makes a tremendous difference in the integrity of the sound, massive. Because you're talking about a long cable running at a mic level versus a line to a hotter level. Obviously you get a better relationship at the console when you're driving those long lines to the higher level.

'On *Bastards*, we went to another studio in the Valley with a Neve room to overdub and they had a limited mic supply, so I just pretty much didn't try to do anything outside of the box. I did do some phasing stuff – not phasing with regard to phasers and effects but I tried to set up a matrix when I mixed to induce a little bit of phase anomaly on the side guitars, just to try and get those guitars as big and out to the side as far as I possibly could.'

Offering his own recollections on the sound the band and producers achieved on *Bastards* with two guitarists, Lemmy recalled in his autobiography that 'we really enjoyed making *Bastards*. Although he was with us for the next album, *Sacrifice*, I really consider it Würzel's last Motörhead record because it was the last one where he was really there in spirit.'

The lead vocals would be a revelation for Howard Benson, who has 'done a lot of really *huge* records since I've worked with Lemmy but I have to give him a lot of credit for being a big influence on my life and career. I have to give him a lot of credit on teaching me how to recognise what I would consider greatness in terms of the ability to not be a pretender. Lemmy is definitely authentic, he's the real deal and, as a record producer, you're always trying to make sure that you have the real deal in there and are not producing people that are faking it. I'm not saying I learned about hit songs from him but I certainly learned about the real deal and I don't think anybody is more authentic than he is.

'If you look at his take on things, he's really obsessed with medieval stuff and English history, so on the first record we were marching in gravel pits to simulate soldiers marching around and all of that stuff for me was just brand new but I also realised, for Lemmy, it was who he was and I had to get into his way of looking at the world at that point.'

Elaborating on his recording process, Benson paid Lemmy another compliment in recollecting that 'when he sings, he sings harmonies almost like they're lead-vocal melody parts, which I think is really cool because I always think his harmonies are almost as strong as his melodies. So when you listen to the first song on the *Bastards* LP, I remember the harmony being unbelievably cool because he sang a major second harmony, which is very hard to do when you're singing harmonies to sing a step above the main vocal. Because it's not like a third or fifth, it's like a second above it, so when he was singing it – the whole vocal harmony – I was thinking to myself, how is he pulling this off? Because it's so hard to do that but he's very bright when it comes to that kind of stuff. He knows what he likes in the studio, that's the thing about Lemmy, so he's, in some ways, easy to produce.

'But sometimes when you try to push him to grow a little bit, he is what he is, so you really have to have a good reason for him to do something different musically that you want him to try. He has pluses and minuses – the pluses are that Lemmy knows who he is; the minuses are that he sometimes might not want to try some things that other artists might want to try.'

Ryan Dorn spotted something similar in the recording process. 'It's all about that patented Lemmy vocal, which always would save the song,' he confirms. 'When you have a song there that is just sort of "meat and potatoes" – what they're about – and you put that vocal on it, it's like, "OK, this sounds like Motörhead".'

In recording the legend, producer Howard Benson recalls, 'We used a C12 on Lemmy. We really used any mic we could to downplay some of the top end and growly stuff that is naturally in his voice, so we wanted to bring out a bit more warmth to it. He's one of the best rock singers I've ever worked with.'

As work on the album's recording entered the mixing stages, the producer adds, 'One thing about *Bastards* that's notable is it's probably one of the first of their records that had ever really used the computer. We recorded a lot of that record with Turtle Beach digital editing software to make the songs tighter and better, and Motörhead's was one of the first albums that technology was used on.' Expanding on the latter aspect of the team's mixing process with the band, engineer Ryan Dorn recalls that 'that was Howard's little baby, he was always the tinkerer. He had this software, back before I even had a computer, I would go on the internet with. But he had this Turtle Beach PC software that was basically a stereo mastering program or editor that could do a lot of corrective stuff with regard to pitch and editing that was very cool. So Howard would bring the finished mixes home before mastering and he would tinker.'

In sum, Lemmy, as he shared in his autobiography, felt that 'Howard really liked being our producer... We did argue quite a bit while we were in the studio though, me and him. Early on in our working relationship, there was one day where I'd been waiting around for endless hours while he was going over some guitar part or something. So I finally got a hamburger and I was just starting to eat it when he said, "Right! Vocals!" "Oh, you cunt!' I said, "Why don't you let me eat my fucking hamburger?" But no – "Come on, come on, we're on a deadline!" Howard was being a bitch in the studio, you know. So I did the logical thing: I shoved the burger's contents into the mixing board. I figured it was fair...

'[Ultimately, I think] *Bastards* was one of the best albums we ever did... He really wanted this album and we gave it to him and, amazingly enough, he stayed with us for the four albums. I don't know how he managed to break the two-album barrier but he did and we were generally happy with him... He did a great job on *Bastards* – I think it's one of the best albums Motörhead has made so far. Every song is strong… There's "Don't Let Daddy Kiss Me", which is about child abuse. I wrote that one on my own and I'd had it for three years in my pocket… "Death and Glory" and "I Am the Sword" are probably my favourites, along with "Lost in the Ozone".' In interview with www.roughedge.com, Lemmy expanded on his feelings about how the latter track turned out, confirming, 'This is also one of my favourites! Note the panic-stricken bass solo. Hear the curious backing vocals from Phil "strangle-throat" Campbell!'

Released on 29 November 1993, *Bastards* garnered critical praise, further acknowledgement of the band's ever-growing legend. *Billboard* celebrated the fact that 'underground heroes Motörhead thankfully returned to a more familiar sonic formula (extremely loud and fast) on the excellent *Bastards*… This album remains one of the band's strongest releases in the 1990s.' *Rolling Stone* praised the 'hard edge of self-explanatory rockers like "Born to Raise Hell"'. Rounding out that glowing commentary, album producer Howard Benson adds, 'One thing I will say is, when we ended up with *Bastards*, that was a really, really great record that ended up standing up to the test of time. And I think a lot of it was just because Lemmy did open himself up to a little bit of help from me, so the record was better because the arrangements were solid and things like that. So I think, in some ways, when he listened back to *Bastards* he really wanted to work with me again. And so I asked myself, do I want to live or die? And, ultimately, I decided I'd try it again and we were successful for the next three or four records.'

Lemmy himself agreed, hailing the album in an interview with www.kt2.com as up there in contention for 'the greatest album we've ever recorded. The songwriting, the production, the playing, the effort we put into it. I think it's perfect.'

Throughout the first half of the 1990s, Lemmy — between sessions writing Motörhead material — also found time to lend his lyric-writing talent to Ozzy Osbourne, penning the hit singles 'Mama I'm Coming Home' and 'See You On the Other Side'. He told *Inked* magazine about how the collaboration came about. 'Just after I moved to the States, Sharon rang up and said, "Can you write four songs for me?" and made me an offer I couldn't refuse. One of them was "Mama I'm Coming Home". I made more money out of those four songs than I did in fifteen years with Motörhead. And then I wrote two more for *Ozzmosis*.' Of the writing process, Lemmy told Nina C Alice for www.hardradio.com, 'I never really sat down in a room with him and wrote a song... Ozzy sends me a tape with wordless noises where he wants the vocals and... I'd write them and send them back to him... Sometimes he gives me a story line, sometimes not. 'See You on The Other Side' is about [guitarist] Randy [Rhoads]. He was my friend too.'

Ultimately, though Lemmy wrote six sets of lyrics for Osbourne, including 'Desire' and 'I Don't Wanna Change the World', he recalled, 'They had too much material. Most albums aren't that good because they have too little material but Ozzy had so many songs, they couldn't decide what to put on it.' Luckily for Lemmy, two of the songs selected by team Ozzy were among the biggest smash hits of his solo career, with 'Mama I'm Coming Home' from 1991's *No More Tears* giving Osbourne his only Billboard Top 40 hit, while 'I Don't Want to Change the World' earned him a Grammy for Best Metal Performance.

Chapter Eleven

Sacrifice: 1995

Lemmy – bass, vocals
Phil Campbell – guitar
Würzel – guitar
Mikkey Dee – drums
Producing and mixing – Howard Benson
Producers – Ryan Dorn and Motörhead
Engineering and mixing – Ryan Dorn
Released – 11 July 1995

When Motörhead set about recording what would be
Sacrifice in 1995, it wasn't without doubts in the mind of
producer Howard Benson. 'I remember thinking, maybe I
shouldn't work with them again. Because it was really
tough, the first record. I think I was just trying to survive
them at that point.

'In an article in *Billboard*, I think Lemmy said he liked working with me the most because I argued the best and that's what it's like in the studio with him. You're fighting and arguing with him the entire time because what's most important to him is his music. And he wants it one way and I want it another but that volatility is definitely a part of why I think those records turned out so good. Because I pushed him and I didn't give up, that's the one thing on all the records: I never walked out on him and kept going.

'On the first record, I was so exhausted from working so hard I actually went to the hospital for exhaustion. One day I passed out, almost, because we literally weren't sleeping to finish the album. So I decided after that I wasn't going to kill myself over it – not that he wasn't trying to kill me in the process – but we also realised we made a really good first record together.'

As an insurance policy of sorts to ensure that their second recording collaboration went as smoothly as possible, the producer instituted a 'Motörhead clause' in his contract, 'because Lemmy had a tendency not to show up at the studio, or he'd show up whenever he wanted to and, a lot of times, the producer got stuck with the bill. So producers would put these clauses in that stated that, if the artist didn't show up at the session, the band was responsible for the money and that came up because of Lemmy. So when I started producing that record, I was aware of all that stuff and I was like definitely not going to let that happen to me.'

While *Bastards* had been tracked at A-list studio A&M, co-producer and engineer Ryan Dorn recalls the band doing 'Sacrifice at Cherokee and it was a very difficult record for me because I just could not wrap my head around trying to get a good drum sound out of that room, because it was *not* A&M by any sense of the word. But there were a lot of technical issues with that record, a lot of things didn't work and, just from an engineering perspective, it was a very frustrating project. I know the budget for *Sacrifice* was not great, I think it was a third of the budget that *Bastards* was, which made doing a record that much more difficult.'

And yet, Lemmy wrote in his autobiography, '*Sacrifice* is one of my favourite records of ours, especially considering the difficulties that were going on behind it. Howard was producing us again but he'd also just gotten an A&R gig with a label called Giant. So his mind was in at least two or three different places and half the time the engineer, Ryan Dorn, was holding it all together, following the direction Howard gave him.'

But that working relationship seemed to work for Benson. 'Ryan was a great engineer and he had really good patience with Lemmy during a lot of the bass and guitar recording,' reasons the producer. 'Because you know what you want from him but it's hard sometimes because you have to push him a bit, because he likes to do it a certain way. Lemmy's very opinionated and, even if you tell him this way is better and prove its better, it doesn't matter, he still doesn't think it's better. So you really have to prove it to him and, in some ways, I do like that about him, that he was never easy to push around in the studio.'

Dorn was listed on the album as co-producer. 'My getting credited as a co-producer on *Sacrifice* was really me raising my hand and saying, "You know what? I never got credited for co-producing on *Bastards*," and my involvement was the same on all of those records. I'll just throw this out there: most engineers do a lot of producing, they're just not credited as producer and so, on the second record, I raised my hand at that time and said, "You know what, man? I should get a co-production on this one because it really wasn't fair that I didn't get one on the first album." And Lemmy agreed, which was cool of him. Those records were very hard on Howard. I think Lem sort of respected me at a certain level because I was always there giving it a hundred per cent. Howard – like any good producer – is always multi-tasking and doing other things, and I think a lot of times, that pissed Lemmy off, that Howard wasn't necessarily there a hundred per cent of the time.'

Ahead of entering the studio, Dorn had another issue he had to navigate with the band. 'With the *Sacrifice* record, I remember thinking it was going to be a tough record to make because the songs ultimately weren't there,' he remembers. 'The songs were a little self-indulgent and Lem has a tendency as a writer to get a little on the self-indulgent side when I think he's scared and doesn't have something that really can resonate and is viable. It's very easy in those situations to start looking inward to the point where it's almost a comic-book representation of what you see or what your commentary is. Lyrically, I think he could have thought through stuff because half the beauty of what he does is put comedy in motion: it's lean and focused and simple. And that's a process of honing. He starts with something and then he sort of hones it to be as simple as it can be. I don't think it's like he gets an idea and that's what it is.

'And on *Sacrifice* some of those songs were a little rushed and, if he'd taken a little more time with regard to the writing process, I think it would have clarified a lot of things. Let's call a spade a spade: look at the body of work on *Bastards* and then look at the body of work – as far as songs go – on *Sacrifice*, and they just weren't that strong. And I'd equate that to a touring schedule, not necessarily taking the time to write the songs and I don't necessarily think they were ready for another record because, again, I don't think the songs were there.'

Lemmy's viewpoint was very different. As he commented in his autobiography, 'We went in the studio with some great song – we wrote "Sex and Death" in ten minutes on the last day of rehearsal. I changed the lyrics once we were recording but that's always the way it goes. I altered "In Another Time" out of all recognition and I had three sets of lyrics for "Make 'em Blind". That's what's fun about making a record – you go in with one thing and come out with something completely different. I added a part in "Out of the Sun" – I had to because it only had two and a half verses, and who can sing half a fucking verse?' Still, in the same piece, the singer conceded that 'Sacrifice had a lot more nonsense on it than most of the albums before it; the lyrics don't mean anything you can really get a hold of.' In an interview with *MOO* magazine, Lemmy added, 'We do all our albums real quick. [*Sacrifice*] was one of the longer ones. We actually had time to write all the songs before we got into the studio.'

Mikkey Dee's recollection of the process was somewhat different, as he confided to journalist Roger Lotring. '[For the] first two weeks, nothin' happened,' revealed the drummer. 'Out of five weeks, two is a joke and three is harder than you've ever seen anyone work… a sweaty producer hangin' over our fuckin' heads; management calling every night, screaming – it's from one extreme to the other, which is quite fantastic.' Once the band got down to the work of writing the album's songs, continued the drummer, 'me and Phil probably wrote nine riffs out of eleven… We gotta start somewhere and that start is usually me and Phil.' In the same conversation, guitarist Phil Campbell confirmed, 'We do most of it… We leave Lem to the lyrics, bits and pieces… He doesn't like rehearsing or going in on writing [with] us. He just lets us get on with it because he's lazy, y'know? Just any excuse for a day off. We'll put it down and he comes in and does his bit. It's like a team but it's [got] different stages.'

Lemmy expanded on the process in his autobiography.

Top: Fast Eddie, Phil Taylor and Lemmy live on *Top of the Pops* in 1979.

© *Rex Features*

Middle: The same line-up the following year at Hammersmith Odeon.

© *Rex Features*

Right: Producer Jimmy Miller in 1970. He would go on to helm *Overkill* and *Bomber* for Motörhead.

© *Getty Images*

Above: The line-up with Brian Robertson, far right.   © *Rex Features*

Below: Playing on Channel 4's *The Tube* – Würzel, Pete Gill, Lemmy and Phil Campbell.   © *Rex Features*

Top: Eddie Clarke, producer Vic Maile and Lemmy take a break during the recording of 'Iron Fist and the Hordes from Hell' – eventually released as 'Iron Fist' – at Jackson's Studio in Rickmansworth, London, 1981.

Below left: Clarke's Stratocaster and effects unit.

Below right: Back-up guitars for 'Fast' Eddie.

All photographs on this page courtesy of © Chris Harris www.headfirstonly.com

Above: Bassist Bill Laswell produced *Orgasmatron* in 1986.   © *Getty Images*

Below: Motörhead performing in France in 1987.   © *Rex Features*

Above left: Lemmy in 2001. © *Getty Images*

Above right: Bob Kulick produced 2000's *We Are Motörhead*. © *Getty Images*

Below: Lemmy, Mikkey Dee and Phil Campbell with the Grammy Award they picked up for 'Whiplash'. © *Getty Images*

Ozzy Osbourne and Lemmy in 1981 and, *below,* a ceremony for Randy
Rhoads included Ozzy, Dolores Rhoads, Sharon Osbourne and, far right,
Lemmy. Lemmy wrote about Rhoads in his lyrics for Ozzy's 'See You on
the Other Side'.   © *Rex Features*

Above: Phil Campbell and Lemmy live in Brittany in July 2008.

© *Rex Features*

Below: Motörhead live at Guilfest in July 2009.

© *Getty Images*

'Sometimes in the studio something practically comes out of thin air – "Make 'em Blind" was like that. We improvised a lot in the studio and Phil did this brilliant solo in one take. It sounds like it's being played backwards but he played it forward and he fell over halfway through it, right over the couch, flat on his back with the fucking guitar, laughing uproariously. We didn't even need to think about doing it again – it was great.' Another song which popped up out of thin air in the studio, remembered Mikkey Dee in his interview with *MOO*, was the record's title track. 'We went in and did this fucker in twenty minutes... [I had this] drum beat I had made, basically during a drum solo with [Don] Dokken.' Phil Campbell added in the same interview that the song 'started off with that Latin thing... It took twenty minutes to write,' with Mikkey noting of the song's construction, 'When we had what we wanted, I went in and did all the drums, and we built it from there... We recorded it, just guitars and drums, then played it for Howard and Lem, and said, "All right, just sit down... take a deep breath and see what you think about this." And I remember Lem said, "What the hell is this?"'

In an interview with journalist Al Harbison, Lemmy described 'Sex and Death' as having an 'unsafe, vicious rhythm. We had the lyrics written before we wrote the tune. Sex and death; two most important things in life.' Going on to detail the inspiration behind the lyrics for 'War for War', the singer explained, 'That's almost a recruiting song. It's like I've written all these anti-war songs and I keep getting accused of being pro-war, right? So I thought I'd write a pro-war one and see if people come out saying it's an anti-war one. Of wars, WWII is the most interesting one because of the Nazi thing. I just got a new book by this guy who found some archives. It turns out that the head of the Gestapo was supposedly killed in Berlin in 1945. Well, they dug up his grave a few years ago and there were three people in it. None of them were him. He has apparently been working for the CIA since 1948.'

Once pre-production had concluded and principle recording began, Mikkey Dee told *MOO* magazine, 'I was done in a day and a half in the studio.' He might have found drum tracking quick and easy but it was very different for Ryan Dorn. 'Getting a good drum sound was challenging, starting with the room – which, for that kind of music, I think, was too live. Mikkey Dee hits the drums like he's killing them, he truly is a drummer that hits things for a living; the guy is relentless. And I think that room was too live of a room, so you wind up getting all this clouding in the mid-range, and your separation and everything got murky. It was a weird record because it was bright yet it was dull and everything from the tape machine wasn't as great. The console was a Trident A-Range, which had been modified and was not being properly maintained. I knew because I had worked on that board three or four years prior. And that board, when properly maintained, sounded great but I think it was a question of deferred maintenance on that desk. The tape machine was wacky – it wasn't a Studer 800, it might have been an Atari.

'What we focused on getting on that was great drums, and I know that sounds kind of bizarre, and know a lot of people that have worked with them differently but, at that time, all I was focused on was getting the greatest useable drum sound and, if we happened to get a keeper bass or guitar take in the process, great but the focus was getting the best-sounding drums out of that room as possible. I would say we went back and did overdubs on ninety per cent of the stuff. That was not a live record.'

Elaborating on the latter, producer Howard Benson recalls that, during recording for the bed tracks, 'I had the band track through pods and DI stuff through simple set-ups because I knew I wasn't keeping a lot of it, because the only thing I was really going for was the drums, because the guitar amps are very complicated set-ups and you can't get that all at once when you're trying to track, so we weren't worried much about that stuff at the time.'

Once drums had been tracked, Dorn recalls, the band next 'went into this cave in the back, which was just the most depressing place in the world to work, it was horrible. We did all the overdubs and all of the vocals in there and it was really dreadful, a horrible place to work, I can't even begin to tell ya. Those were long days and it's not like Lemmy likes to sit in the hammock and sip piña coladas but everybody likes a little sunshine in their life, and that room was *way* in the back of the studio, it was a little tiny dungeon. I think

Howard ultimately regretted saying, "OK, we're gonna work here," but I think the budget dictated he had to do it. Nobody likes working in a U-Boat and that was a pretty depressing place. It affected me certainly because there was something about that room that was very difficult to work in. I've talked to other people about it and they said, "Oh God, you were in that room, oh God, you poor bastard." So it really, really was a tough room to work in.'

Once attention had turned to overdubbing, they began with the reliably unique process of capturing Lemmy's bass sound on tape. Lemmy's Rickenbacker, says his producer, 'is very bright, it sounds almost like a guitar. He's playing through two Marshall guitar amps. If you listen to any of those records, there's not a lot of bottom end on a lot of his records. He likes mid-range because he plays everything like a guitar so, when you watch him play bass, it's like he's playing a guitar part – two strings at once, a lot of times. So he's constantly wanting to hear more mid-range. It's almost maddening at times because you want to put more low-end on there but he doesn't like low-end and is constantly wanting to turn the mids up. So what happens is you end up with guitars and bass in the same range, which gives it the Motörhead sound and is part of why it sounds so interesting, is that he just likes that mid-rangy sound.

Co-producer Ryan Dorn echoes his partner. 'Lemmy's sound was so bright and so ripping that there was actually always more fundamental bottom octave in the guitar tone than there was the bass tone. I think a lot of people have always tried to deal with it in the studio by trying to sneak a DI in or to boost something to try to get some bottom-end element out of his tone. And if you're tracking his bass sound and he doesn't like what he hears, he'll stop and give you shit. He doesn't want to hear a lot of bottom on his bass, he wants it to be ripping and in your face. So instead of fighting it, I ultimately just said, "Well, let's not fight it, let's really look at how they sound live and sort of call the bass a bass without a lot of bottom and try to get a lot of fundamental bottom out of the kick drum and out of the bottom of the rhythm guitars.' And so we had that bass float underneath and right up with the lead vocal, almost treating it like a lead instrument. Lemmy's bass tone is what it is and that's why it works.'

It was, after all, a bass sound that Lemmy had perfected by 20 years of playing, as he himself pointed out to *Moo* magazine. 'I play a lot of notes but I also play a lot of chords. And I play a lot of open strings. I just don't play like a bass player. There are complaints about me from time to time. It's not like having a bass player; it's like having a deep guitarist… [My stacks are] old Marshalls and Superbass JMP IIs 'cause I don't like those JCM800s.'

Offering his own observations on working with Kilmister's sound stylistically in the studio, producer Howard Benson shares that 'Lemmy loved Bo Diddley and stuff like that, that he heard growing up on BBC Radio and, if he had his way, he would probably make "Johnny B

Goode" and, if you really strip his songs down, that's really
what they are, just good old American rock'n'roll,
interpreted by him. A lot of people don't really realise that
but we used to joke about it in the studio; the guitarist
would go, "Another Bo Diddley song," which meant it was
a I-IV-V progression and very simple, with a galloping bass
part and that's what Lemmy naturally liked to do.'

Aside from bass, Dorn revealed that Lemmy 'is a multi-
instrumentalist, he doesn't just play bass. So on "Don't Let
Daddy Kiss Me" and "Lost in the Ozone", Lemmy played
both of those on acoustic guitar. I think he can play drums
too, although Mikkey Dee would never let him sit behind
the kit because Mikkey's an incredibly fabulous drummer.
But for those acoustic guitars, I always used multiple mics –
not necessarily to create a stereo feel but to have as many
microphones as possible because, when it comes time to
mix, you never knew if that one mic choice you'd made was
wrong for what you'd had going on. So my typical thing
with an acoustic set-up then, and I still do it when I'm doing
rock-acoustic, is to use either a 451 or KM84 right where
the fret meets the neck, really close, then an 87 kind of
parked above approximately where the player's head is but
looking at the guitar. And then I'll actually do a couple of
stereo room mics and that pretty much covers my base for
whatever I'd need to do when I mix.'

Covering other unusual instrumentation in context of the
traditional Motörhead album, Dorn explains, 'Howard
played some ancillary piano parts on Motörhead you

probably can't hear because they're buried underneath the wall of everything else.'

Production soon reached the point of guitar overdubbing, as co-producer Ryan Dorn remembers. 'Tuning was a bit of an issue for those guys because they're used to rockin' live, so the studio is a different animal because every time we hit stop we're like, "Check your tuning," so that became a bit of a laborious process. When we were tracking the album's guitar overdubs, Phil's always Phil; the charming thing with Phil is, again, he's a little scatterbrained and is always bringing new guitars to try out, and I remember there being a lot of intonation issues on that record, tuning issues, amplifier problems... it was just one of those records that was really technically difficult to pull off. Because the creative process is a very delicate thing, because all of these things need to be going on, on the fringe, that allow you to focus and be creative, and do what it is you do. And when every second you're breaking strings, or an amplifier's blowing tubes, or the mic craps out, or the console breaks, it's like you're driving a car down the freeway jamming on the breaks every ten feet. It was a little disconcerting and I was so glad to get out of there.

'When I was miking those cabinets, I used a 57 and a 421 and, I believe, experimented with some ribbon mics and in the room on a couple things, I believe I used an old Western Electric, which is a hybrid dynamic ribbon mic, the 639, and looks like a giant bullet mic. They're huge. I'm sure I used 87s as well.'

Dorn was a great admirer of Würzel. 'I don't want to paint him as the secret weapon,' says the co-producer, 'but that guy came up with some incredible guitar riffs and was a very, very solid rhythm guitar player.' Still, from the point of view of the rest of the band, as Lemmy recalled in his autobiography, 'it became clearer and clearer every day that Würzel was on his way out of the band. He wouldn't extend himself at all and usually just sat there while we were writing songs, with his guitar across his knees. When we stopped playing, he stopped playing and when we started again, he would too. The whole thing with him seemed like it happened overnight but, of course, it had been building up for a long time. It was very difficult for me because for years he was my best friend in the band and then he became this person I didn't know, and [who] hated me, and that can break your heart.' Phil Campbell added in *Moo* magazine that 'he didn't contribute hardly anything to the writing. He was there when we wrote it but he didn't contribute hardly anything, really. And he did only a couple of solos but he played on the album and he should be credited with it.'

Lemmy began recording his vocal tracks and Ryan Dorn quips that 'with the way Lemmy sings, he puts an 87 up and it's like three and a half or four feet above his mouth, maybe six and a half or seven feet in the air so, when he sings, he actually looks up at the microphone. Now, what's interesting about this is, when he first did this, I was like, "Dude, what are you doing?" Because I'd never seen anyone do that. But when you think about it, what he's doing is: there's a thing called proximity, which is the closer you get on a capsule, the low end and bottom end of the voice become accentuated. But when you're talking about trying to fit a vocal sound into a wall of guitars and that bass tone, if you had this huge vocal sound, it would be very difficult to get those vocals naturally to fit in the track. So what he'd learned over the years is, if you sing off the mic, it has this tendency to make the vocal smaller, therefore allowing it to fit into the track, therefore it doesn't compete with the rhythm guitar. It was a very, very smart way to do it and I learned a lot from him with regard to that. I would always trust Lemmy's instincts. I may look at him from time to time like a deer in the headlights but nine times out of ten, if you trusted him and took what he had to say, or didn't question what he was used to doing, the end result was always very, very cool.'

Principle production wrapped and the team turned to the task of mixing. Co-producer Ryan Dorn perked up. 'We mixed at a place called ARLA in Glendale, which was a fabulous change of pace and place to mix. They had an old SSL in there – it was an E series but one of the very first E series and that console just had a sound. Put it this way, I couldn't wait till we were done recording.'

As usual, the producer recalls, '[Lemmy] was around every day during the mixing sessions for the album. That guy is so dedicated, so unbelievably dedicated. And really one of the greatest, polarising personalities in rock. Those records were very, very, very challenging, exhausting, and a lot of it had to do with Lemmy's polarising personality. You have to understand when you're producing somebody, there's a certain level of trust that the artist has to abdicate to you and say, "OK, you're going to steer the ship and, ultimately, when there's a decision to be made, I'm going to have to defer that to the producer'. And I don't think Lemmy ever one hundred per cent got that: he's a control freak, the alpha-dog. I had never worked with somebody where one moment I was so angered by some of the things that went down, some of his attitude issues and stuff, and the next minute I'd go to war with the guy and fight by his side till I died. Really, he's such a magical human being and he has a lot of flaws but there is no doubt he really is the persona that he puts out to the world. That is not an attitude.'

Mixing progressed and Dorn cites one of his greater technical challenges being that of overcoming the sonic limitations of Cherokee. 'At that time, I know I was running drum samples, I don't know how loud they were. The problem with drum samples with Mikkey Dee is his kick-drum patterns are double bass, and good luck trying to get a sample to follow that and sound natural. So, ultimately, it was "let's look intrinsically at what we have on tape, what's good and let's play up those strengths and try to put a Band-aid on those things that were ultimately not up to par", is what it was.'

Once mixing wrapped, the band appeared to be quite

happy with the results. Mikkey Dee told *Moo* magazine, '*Sacrifice* is a very good album. I tell you what, all the albums have been really, really good. I don't say that because I play on them but I think they… see, I keep saying this… if I do an album, I don't want to take two or three steps forward every year. If we only take one step or half a step every year it's good, as long as we don't go backwards. As long as we don't start to sound like we're copying ourselves. Each album is so different from the other but it's still the same, it's still kind of the same Motörhead… you won't get a better album than ours.'

Lemmy, in a conversation with journalist Al Harbison, cited his favourite track on the album as 'Over Your Shoulder'. 'I think it is the best written song on the CD. I think it will be the next single.'

Released on 11 July 1995, *Sacrifice* was a critical darling, as usual, with *Billboard* pointing out that while 'metal bands are supposed to lose their energy and power as they age… Motörhead stubbornly refused to obey that rule, maintaining their string of tough, enjoyable albums into the mid-1990s. *Sacrifice* [is] straight ahead, breakneck-fast, ear-shatteringly loud Motörhead, with buzzing guitars, near-martial rhythms and surprisingly catchy hooks… On the whole it's a thoroughly engaging and entertaining record from one of the most consistent metal bands in history.'

Producer Ryan Dorn seemed to disagree. 'When you put that record in compared to *Bastards*, *Bastards* is just huge sounding, still to this day, it's just an awesome-sounding record,' he says. 'I think *Sacrifice* sounds a little small and that's not to say it doesn't fit the music. I think it sounds more like they sound if you were to listen to them live: shredding, blowing your ears out in the rehearsal space. Because in a live situation, those guys had it, their tone was dialled in. Mickey's a great drummer, and Lemmy can sing all day and do what Lemmy does fearlessly, ultimately that's what makes them charming. Ultimately, it's got this certain energy to it but it, by no sense of the words was, technically, a great-sounding rock record. I think we looked at what we had and tried to make the best of what we had, and kind of lucked out and got something that was cool. But I just walked away thinking, God, if we'd cut it at A&M, we could have pushed the envelope that much farther.'

The band's next LP would be the first in almost a decade without rhythm guitarist Würzel who, Lemmy recalled in a conversation with *Moo*, departed the band after 'he played two solos [on *Sacrifice*]: "Dogface Boy" and "Out of the Sun" and he did rhythm guitar on the other tracks as well… [But] he was getting worse. At the end he was hardly playing. He only did two solos on the last album. Before, him and Phil would have been fighting for each solo… Familiarity bred contempt, as it so often does… He quit a week and a half before we went out on tour in Europe… He just upped and split.'

Looking towards future albums, Lemmy revealed that

'the next one is going to be slightly more like *Bastards* than *Sacrifice*. We've got three ideas for songs already.' Mikkey Dee, for his own part in an interview with *Big Shout*, added, 'All I can say about the next album is that I want it to be the hardest motherfucking Motörhead album ever made. I want it to be stone hard. Fuck the melodic shit. It's going to be super-hard. I love this album but the next one's going to be super-hard.'

Chapter Twelve

Overnight Sensation: 1996

Lemmy – bass, vocals, harmonica on track 2, acoustic guitar on tracks 5 and 11

Phil Campbell – guitar

Mikkey Dee – drums

Producers – Howard Benson and Duane Barron

Producers – Ryan Dorn and Motörhead

Mixing – Ryan Dorn and Duane Barron

Released – 15 October 1996

Prior to heading without Würzel into the studio to record 12th studio LP, *Overnight Sensation*, as Lemmy recounted in his autobiography, 'Mikkey and I figured we needed to get somebody else. But then Phil said, "I'd like to try it on my own." So we decided to carry on as a three-piece and see how it went, and it turned out to be amazing… To be honest, I'm glad we're a three-piece again. For one thing, it saved us having to find another guitar player! But also, as I've said before, when there are two guitar players, you can never get things worked out completely because somebody won't agree with it. With one guitar player, the bass can do anything... [Phil's also] a natural when it comes to playing guitar. Phil can be in any condition and he'll still play you a good solo. He just does it instinctively... Phil picks up a guitar and it practically becomes part of his body... Motörhead has always worked really great as a trio... (And still does today.)

'If there's two guitars, you have to sort of tow the line a bit because, if the two guitarists ain't together – and the bass too, of course! – it's really messy. But with only one guitar player, you can do anything.'

Drummer Mikkey Dee, in an interview with *Drum God*, gave his view about the departure of the fourth member. 'It was easier because Würzel was not happy in the band... I gotta say I love Würzel... Würzel, I used to say, was more Motörhead than me, Phil and Lemmy together. He was a true Motörheader, you know. He wrote super-hard songs and riffs, and I miss that sometimes. 'Cause me and Phil, we might sometimes write a little too... not soft but maybe too "musically-corrected" songs, where Würzel was very simple, straight, very hard riffs. Nothing complicated with him whatsoever. It was so fucking great. So I miss that sometimes, yes. But, no, it wasn't harder, it was actually easier when it actually happened.'

As the band worked through pre-production without Würzel, reorientating their power to channel through a three-piece band, Lemmy, in an interview with *MOO* and www.hardradio.com, said he felt 'we sound better... y'know; more controlled power now... It's certainly got more power. It sticks to the beat a lot better... Phil is definitely playing great. Mikkey is a monster.' Lemmy wrote in his autobiography, of the album, 'We spent four weeks writing it and four weeks in the studio... did some European festivals and when we came back we were in the studio another month or so. It generally takes us about three months to do a record and this one was no different – it's just that those three months were a little spread out! We hired Howard again as producer but Duane Barron came in and did a lot of work under Howard's direction. Then Howard came in at the mix and sorted it all out. Duane was all right – you could tell he liked guitar!'

Baron, for his own part, recalls of coming aboard to work on the new Motörhead album, 'I was brought in to co-produce the record with Howard because Howard was busy and me and Ryan worked together on it, and I was there for the whole thing, pretty much top to bottom. The recording process was fairly normal; we didn't have a huge budget.' Of Baron's addition to the production team, producer Ryan Dorn felt, 'Sweet guy, great guy to work with, we had fun.'

Pre-production got underway and co-producer Duane Baron explains, 'I'd work on the arrangements with the guys and Howard would come down to check them over and okay them. In pre-production, usually the songs tell me what to do and their stuff was pretty together. The band would work on music separately and then Lemmy would be in the back room of the studio eating his Ruffles sour cream chips, working on lyrics. Then he'd bring me the lyrics and have Howard and I read them over, and we'd give him a thumbs up, or make suggestions on changes, and sometimes he wouldn't take kindly to that, sometimes he'd be open and that was our process all throughout recording. Lemmy is the kind of guy that has a book full of lyrics without necessarily any music written to them, so he'll just give you his book of lyrics, and you'd sit down and read through them like a book of poetry. He always had tons of lyrics on him and we'd just work together to give him feedback on which worked best for the record.'

The course of Lemmy's lyric writing didn't always run smoothly. 'I might get blocked but it doesn't last longer than a couple of days,' he admitted to *Chart* magazine. 'That's what I've been doing all this time, is writing songs. I'm pretty good at it now… I write words all the time but we write songs in rehearsals before the recording. It's if the mood strikes you. Sometimes you write nothing and sometimes you write twenty-five and only use five… I amuse the shit out of myself sometimes. When I was writing "I Won't Pay Your Price" [from *Overkill*], I fell off my chair laughing: "Don't stop me / Don't even try / Gonna stick my finger in your eye." It was fuckin' hilarious.' He revealed some of his specific favourites in an interview with *WILMA* magazine. '*Overnight Sensation* has some songs like "Don't Believe a Word" that started out boring but it got really good. I like "Broken" a lot too.' Still, as happy as Lemmy and company might have been with the album's songs, producer Ryan Dorn recalled feeling déjà vu. 'Once again, here we go, this is the downward spiral with regard to bringing songs to the table. One could argue that, if *Sacrifice* was a little light in the songs department, *Overnight Sensation* was a step down, as *Sacrifice* was to *Bastards*. I don't know what inspires Lemmy to write, I just think the songs, ultimately, were not there.'

Heading into principle recording, Lemmy felt a certain ease in the recording environment. 'I like the studio a lot more than I used to because I know what's going on a lot more. I've learned what you can do. I don't know exactly how to turn the knobs. The studio sound of Motörhead has gotten a lot fiercer. People think that the old recordings were harder but they're not. It's just that they were hard when you first heard them because of what was around then.' Ryan Dorn was not as happy about the set-up. 'I think the budget for this record was $1 and we recorded at some place in the Valley that had no reason to be a recording studio, ultimately. A shitty drum room and shitty Atari tape machine that took for ever to load, it was just dreadful. So we were just dealing with the semantics of trying to work around the fact that, again, the songs were not there. So I went into it with the attitude of "let's try to make the best record we can" and I think everybody did the best they could.'

Offering fans insight into recording for the first time in over a decade as a three-piece in the studio, Lemmy wrote in his autobiography, 'This was our first official album as a three-piece since *Another Perfect Day* with Robbo. If you're wondering what that was like – it went the same as a four-piece except one guy wasn't there! Or the same as the Everly Brothers plus one. It was a bit more fraught but that was just because Phil, being the only guitarist, felt that there was a lot riding on his shoulders... So he was under some added pressure but he proved himself well. *Overnight Sensation* was a great album for him. Mikkey was his usual perfect self – he always finishes his drum tracks well ahead of schedule. This time around he did them in one day.' From his technical standpoint, Baron agrees with Lemmy's assessment. 'We cut the drums at Ocean Studios in Burbank. Mikkey, I think he's just incredible. To be honest with you, I think he's one of the best drummers I've ever worked with. I'd put him up there with anybody. The guy's just incredible. Tracking on that part of the record went so fast because Mikkey's so good, he just breezed through the tracks. We did it on a weekend and Howard was there for the drum tracking. I got the drum sound on that record and miked Mikkey's kit up with 421s on the toms, a 57 and a 451 on the snare, and he had two heads on the kicks, a front head and a back head on both his kick drums with a hole just big enough to put a mic through on both of them, and then each kick was outer-miked on the front head.'

As attention turned to the album's overdubbing, recording

moved to Track House Recording Studios. Of the album's heavier moments, Lemmy commented in an interview with www.hardradio.com/ *WILMA*, 'I did that acoustic playing. It's not a new voice, it's just a voice I haven't used in a while... You know, the bass is still under that acoustic guitar, you never lose it. It's just a change of mood.'

Not surprisingly, Duane Baron had to face the usual Motörhead-producer's hurdle in tracking the singer's bass sound. 'Obviously, Lemmy's bass was a challenge to record because it sounds like a guitar. It's really bright and thin, and usually when you started adding bottom end to it he would get pissed off, so you had to kind of sneak it in. That was definitely not one of his favourites because he likes it real big and distorted. It was very unique, in my experience, that he played out of a Marshall cabinet.'

When it came to Campbell's guitar, Baron found it easier to record the rhythm over the lead tracks. 'I think Phil's great, he's got his own style. He reminds me of like a Mick Mars, stronger on the rhythms. He wants to be a virtuoso on lead but I don't think he's necessarily there. I think sometimes he was a little on the insecure side because he would go over and over and over on his leads but, again, not everybody has to be Eddie Van Halen, so he was fine. He's great, he's got his own vibe. He worked on a song or two a day and usually did leads after rhythms, and the whole process took a couple weeks.'

Once attention turned to Lemmy's lead-vocal tracking, 'we'd do vocals first thing when he'd come in and he's the type of guy that, if it's worked for him before, he tends to do it again, so that schedule worked for him. As the night goes on, Lemmy gets more difficult but during the day he's pretty easy to work with. The only challenging thing doing vocals with Lemmy was he's very impulsive, so he can get impatient, so there were times when he'd pop up off the couch and say, "I'm ready to do the vocal now," and we'd say, "Lemmy, we have to get a compressor level happening," and he'd just want to do it now and, if we made him do something over and over, and do a few tracks, he'd ask, "What's wrong with that?" And as a producer you'd just have to say, "Trust me, do it again," and as he starts trusting you, he's much easier.

'But building that initial trust between us was the hardest part of doing vocals on that album. Because when you're first starting out and you tell him something like "you need to do it again" and he asks, "What's wrong with that?" and then, as time goes on and you prove to him that you know what you're talking about, he's easier to work with. Having said that, he was pretty consistent with his words. Lemmy's a very good lyricist. Howard worked on some of the vocal tracks with Lemmy but Ryan and I did most of the engineering. When Lemmy's doing his vocals, he doesn't like a whole lot of people around, just him and the producers.'

As production on the album wound down, Kilmister acknowledged in an interview that the album was 'recorded under a bit of pressure', with Baron recalling of the mixing process, 'I was there to give my two cents but Ryan was pretty much the engineer on that part of the album's recording. Howard was around for all the mixing but Ryan really had a *lot* to do with the mixing because he, by that point, had been brought in on the boards because, again, Lemmy likes working with people he's worked with before and he felt comfortable with Ryan being there, given it was my first time working with Motörhead. So Howard and I were there for balances and stuff. I remember playing a lot of chess with Lemmy – he's actually really good. So while Ryan was setting up the mixes, Lemmy and I would play chess all afternoon, sitting in the room and listening to the mixes.' Asked to single out one of his favourite moments, Lemmy told www.hardradio.com that he'd go for 'Broken', which 'sounds like a come-out-you're-surrounded voice… they did that in the studio while mixing.'

Howard Benson felt he'd learned a great number of invaluable lessons from his experiences in the studio with Motörhead. 'I think it was pivotal for me to do those records and don't think I would have been as good a producer without working with Motörhead. When I see pretenders – that being artists that aren't really true artists – a lot of times in my mind, I subconsciously compare them to Lemmy because I know when you're in the room with him and he's playing bass, he gets up there, plugs in and that thing is so fucking loud that he just rocks, and there is nothing between him and that song. It's complete emotion and what are we selling here? We're selling emotion, not perfection and that's probably what I learned from him more than anything else. I came into that being a bit of a perfectionist and came out of it feeling it was less about being perfect and more about emotion. And I credit Lemmy a lot for that – it was hard to learn but well worth it because I apply it every day in my producing career.'

Released on 15 October 1996, *Billboard* noted of the new album that, 'following the extremely thrashy *Sacrifice*, Motörhead returned to their typical three-chord rock'n'roll onslaught on 1996's *Overnight Sensation*. Also the band's most eclectic in years, its tracks range from pedal-to-the-metal stompers like "Civil War" and "Eat the Gun" to mid-paced groovers like "Listen to Your Heart" (featuring acoustic guitars — shock!) and the classy "I don't Believe a Word". Always a great lyricist, vocalist/bassist Lemmy takes it up a notch with the highly ironic title track and what is quite possibly the band's greatest song of the decade, the exceptionally funny "Crazy Like a Fox"… This wonderfully raw and honest record is guaranteed to please, especially older fans.' In that spirit, Lemmy, in an interview with *Chart*, shared that 'after I die, there'll be no Motörhead because you couldn't get a singer to do this or play bass like that. You probably could but it wouldn't really work. Mikkey Dee is like that. Phil Campbell is almost there too. People that you just can't replace. I'll continue until I drop fuckin' dead.'

Chapter Thirteen

Snake Bite Love/We Are Motörhead: 1998-2000

Snake Bite Love (1998)

Lemmy – bass, vocals

Phil Campbell – guitar

Mikkey Dee – drums

Producers – Howard Benson and Motörhead

Engineer – Mark Dearnley

Released – 10 March 1998

We Are Motörhead (2000)

Lemmy – bass, vocals

Phil Campbell – guitar

Mikkey Dee – drums

Producers – Motörhead, Bob Kulick, Bruce Bouillet and Duane Barron.

Engineer – Bill Cooper

Released – 16 March 2000

'*Snake Bite Love* came together like our albums usually do,'
Lemmy wrote in his autobiography. 'Six weeks before we
recorded it, we didn't even have one song. But when it
came time, we put it together very quickly. Unfortunately,
I was sick for some of the rehearsals and, when you leave
two guys together who aren't singers, you end up with
some weird arrangements. So a couple of songs,
"Desperate for You" and "Night Side" have odd structures.
It's really tricky getting it all to sort of fit together. And, of
course, a lot of things can get changed around in the studio.
The title track started life as a completely different song.
Mikkey put the drum track on with a totally different set
of chords. Then he went back to Sweden, and Phil came in
one day and said, "I'm sick of this one. I don't like it
already." And I said, "Yeah, you're right." So he went in and
came up with a completely new riff, and the whole thing
changed! That album is also a prime example of me writing
the words at the last minute – you know, lazy son of a bitch
one more time, right? But we got it done.'

As a consequence of the latter, Lemmy conceded in a
website interview, 'I went in blind, you know. Writing
frantically on bits of paper all over the studio. So it was
more under the hammer. But then, as we've seen in the
past, Motörhead works better under the hammer… We're
always panicked because we're always under the hammer.
We're very lazy in rehearsing. We never have anything
ready. We pretend to rehearse, then we go to the studio and
we're trapped at the console with the producer glaring and

people looking at their watches going, "Oh, we'd better order some more time." "No, man, it's OK. Don't worry. Jesus Christ!"'

Lemmy explained how he shaped the album's new material in interview with journalist David L Wilson. 'We just try to change a little bit here and there, and I think that we have managed to do that on most albums. *Sacrifice* was different from the one before it and *Overnight Sensation* was different. They are all different in their own way. They all have got stuff that we haven't done before, at least one or two songs.' Expanding in further depth in an interview with the band's main fansite, he reasoned, 'If we were just rewriting the old stuff over and over like some bands do, you know what I mean, I wouldn't even bother. But every album we make is something completely different that nobody really thought we could even do, you know. So I'm quite happy. And we keep bringing the changes. We had organ on this album and we had harmonica for the first time on the last one, you know. And we are a good band too, I think.'

Still, for all the new elements the band introduced on *Snake Bite Love*, in the same interview, Lemmy was quick to reassure fans. 'We got the classic Motörhead sound on there to like "Better Off Dead". I mean, we always played rock'n'roll songs right from the first records. We always played rock'n'roll. So whatever we play becomes Motörhead music anyway.' Offering some specific examples of changes in effect among the band's players, Lemmy, in an interview with the

Columbus Dispatch, cited his playing as 'the background rhythm guitar on the verses of "Dead and Gone"'.

Once the band began tracking, Lemmy recalled in an interview with the *Onion* that they took 'about six weeks in the studio' and engineer Mark Dearnley was tasked with miking Mikkey Dee's drums. 'I had a D112 mic set up on the kick, SM57s both overtop and underneath the snare, a KM84 on the hi-hat, 421s on the toms, C12s on the overheads and a U87 figure-eight dead-side pointed toward the kick for ambience.' As he got to miking Lemmy's bass, Dearnley quips, 'There's study in itself. It's really a distorted guitar sound played on a bass. It works great live when slammed through a PA but is a bit of a problem if you want a balanced tone in your mix – probably not something that Lemmy wants to achieve anyway! I miked his bass cabinet with an RE20 and recorded Lemmy's bass through direct input.'

Elaborating on his truly unique bass sound and style, Lemmy told the *Onion* that, when he's tracking, 'Mikkey's murderous on drums... [so] I just hit the bass very hard... I play like hell on wheels and I'm good at what I do.' Elaborating further on his miking strategies for Lemmy, Dearnley shares, 'I believe that I took a direct feed in addition to Lemmy's studio sound and used the low end from that in order to keep the *noise* (said lovingly) balanced with some low end. As engineers we try to get a balanced sound that works at all volumes but does anyone (other than me) listen to Motörhead quietly? I have a picture from the sessions that Lemmy signed "louder, you bastard!", referring to my modest monitoring levels.'

Attention turned to Phil Campbell's overdubs and the engineer details his set-up for the guitarist's rig. 'Shure SM57s pointed at the speaker, close to the grill, at the junction of the inner and outer cones, a Sennheiser 421 about 45 degrees to the cabinet (perpendicular to and facing the outer cone). Additionally, the 421 has a 1.6k-hertz lift and is compressed heavily, then slowly fed into an even balance of the SM57s until perfection is achieved!'

As on most of his albums, Lemmy composed many of the lyrics in the studio and cited the title track as an example in interview with the *Onion*. 'That was one of those things I wrote in ten minutes, like a stream-of-consciousness thing. Phil changed the chords around on this drum track 'cause that was a different song before and we had it down. It wasn't really happening. Phil went in early one day and listened to the drum track without the guitar and changed it completely. Then I came in and he baffled me with it for ten minutes. It was a great little work and I was just like, "In the jungle... in the jungle..." It was really quick.' In the same interview, he revealed, 'I wrote three different sets of lyrics for "Don't Lie to Me". I wrote four different sets of lyrics for "Joy of Labour". I just couldn't get a couple of them to sound right and I got 'em in the end. It's one of the best albums we've made, I think. We don't do much filler, Motörhead. I mean, we only come up with the amount of tracks we need and don't do filler.'

During tracking of Lemmy's lead vocal tracks, Mark Dearnley recalls, 'We used a Shure SM7 for Lemmy's vocals on "Snake Bite Love". Lemmy has his own mic technique that works well for him. He has the mic above him pointing down at about forty-five degrees and he stretches up to reach it. I don't recall how many takes were made but I don't imagine it was many. Normally, we would take two or three performances and then make a comp [composite].'

It was at this point in the process that producer Duane Baron made his entrance. 'I was just called in to work on the vocals because Lemmy likes working with people he's familiar with… I believe he called Howard and Howard, in turn, called me because he couldn't do it. We did vocals during the day but then there were times, too, when we'd be working at night and, if he felt like singing, he'd go in the booth but, from what I recall, mid-afternoon to late afternoon is commonly when he'd do his vocals. I remember that being fairly pleasant but a lot of it had to do with the relationship. *Snake Bite* was fine and a lot easier than on the first one. I did all the vocal tracking with him on that one and we'd usually have all the lyrics agreed to before he went into track. I had gotten the music in advance and scratch vocals and stuff, so I was pretty much ready to go on what I thought and it was fairly easy. Lemmy was very good with harmonies – he'll come up with harmonies that you wouldn't even think of, he's really good at that. You just sort of let him fly on that and let him do his thing. Because he comes up with these notes that I swear you wouldn't think of.'

Lemmy confided in his autobiography that the record 'came out quite nicely'. Mikkey Dee, in an interview with the band's main fansite, explained that he wasn't quite so delighted with the results. 'We really needed more time for that... That's the album that all three of us said we could have had two more, three more weeks and then had so much more potential for that album. We were stressed out of our minds when we did that album. It turned out OK but no more than OK. That's the album where we all say it's a good album but it's definitely OK. We all know it — we should've had three more weeks on that and it would've been a great album. I blame it completely on the time we had. For instance, we put on the worst song we ever had, which is "Night Side" — it's the worst shit we've ever done and we thought it was shit when we did it. We had no time to write another tune, we had nothing left. I remember me and Phil, we were drained. Our manager called and said, "Mick, you have to write maybe two or three more songs," and I said, "I can't even write one riff more, I'm exhausted." My mind was blank and Lemmy was right, we all went blank. We said, "We need more time, we have to stop and take off for two or three weeks and come back, and it's going to be a world of difference. Let's go and do a couple of shows in California or something. Book us at a couple clubs, $500, I don't give a shit, let's just play a couple shows. Let's take off, let's go swimming for four or five days. I want to go to Mexico for the weekend, anything to get away from the studio." But we had no time to even give that a chance. So we all feel the same way about that album. I've heard people say, "That's the best album you've got," and I'm like, "What planet are you from?"

Billboard appeared to concur, noting in its review of the album that 'nothing quite compares to Motörhead roaring ahead at full blast but, occasionally, it can result in an undistinguished album. *Snake Bite Love* is one of those. There isn't necessarily anything wrong with the record as it offers a solid set of blistering, heavy rockers that race by at breakneck speed but it doesn't add any new twists to the formula or have particularly memorable songs. *Snake Bite Love* sounds fine as it's playing but very little of it leaves a lasting impression. Many members of the group's cult will probably find it worth a listen.'

As the new millennium dawned, the Motörhead cult had become almost one of personality, of not being 'worried about anyone else, you see', says Lemmy. 'I'm only worried about my band, the rest of them can go fuck off, as far as I'm concerned – you've gotta be like that. I think that's played into our longevity as much as anything else. I think we've done a pretty good job all the way through.'

The first album of the century would be *We Are Motörhead*, recorded over the summer of 1999 at Karo Studios in Brackel, Germany. In an interview with journalist Tom Headbanger, Lemmy contrasted using Pro Tools on computer with the band's earliest efforts in the 1970s. 'Back then we used to play and they'd put mics in front of our amps and they'd run it to tape, and now we play and they put mics in front of our amps and they run it... The technology has changed so much in the last fifteen years. It's another fucking world from what it used to be. The first time I recorded it was on three tracks – one for drums, one for bass, one for guitar... Now I use two tracks for bass – a direct line and a mic on the amp. No digital shit, no compressors. We try to use as little of that crap as possible.'

Once the band regrouped in the States, producer Bruce Bouillet was brought in along with co-producer Bob Kulick for the album's mixing. Bouillet: 'It was always real interesting to mix with Lemmy and I'd used Howard Benson's stuff as kind of a guide because I'd always thought Howard was a great producer, so I used his albums to kind of get a reference on what Lemmy might be satisfied with. Lemmy was in the studio the whole time and would make his suggestions on the overall mixes.

'A couple of points he was a real stickler – every time you'd turn his vocals up, he didn't like that, so he always preferred his vocals a little lower in the mix. From a mixing standpoint, it was kind of tearing me in half because I like vocals louder and Lemmy was real adamant that he wanted his vocals down in the mix more. I guess he felt it was a little more raw that way and, because it was his album, of course I went with what he felt, even though I would have had the vocals a lot louder had it been up to me but I wanted to make the guy happy – he was a legend. Also, with his style of bass playing, he didn't like bottom end at all. His comment was always, "Too boomy, too boomy, too much bass." Ultimately, I was proud of being on anything with those guys because, for me, [to have] the chance to work with anybody who was such an innovator in the music scene... and [Motörhead are] really good people, at the end of the day. A lot of times people would have the misunderstanding that the guys in Motörhead were just a bunch of illiterate, wasted-out-of-their-mind rock'n'rollers from way back in the day and it was just the opposite. Lemmy was smart as a whip, really on top of stuff, very, very quick and intelligent.'

Drummer Mikkey Dee, in an interview with the band's biggest online fansite, shared his feeling that 'We Are Motörhead was extremely hard and fast... You put it on the first time and you think, yeah, yeah, this is Motörhead, I recognise this. I think We Are Motörhead is one of the better ones we've ever done.' And yet, in the same interview, the drummer also declared that, in spite of the fact that 'it sold pretty good... it's probably the weakest album since I joined the band, yes, that's for sure.'

As with past albums, We Are Motörhead wasn't all original material, with Lemmy recalling the process of selecting two cover versions in an interview with Seen magazine. 'Phil wanted to do "Satisfaction" but Mickey and I wanted "God Save the Queen", so it was two against one and we did "God Save the Queen". I always loved the song. The Pistols were a real rock band. Steve Jones is one of the best rhythm guitar players in rock'n'roll. Shame he doesn't do more.'

Elaborating further, in an interview with journalist Essi Berelain, was Phil Campbell. 'We did that and a Twisted Sister cover ["Shoot 'Em Down"], all in one evening.'

In the same interview, Lemmy added, 'Twisted Sister wanted it for some Twisted Sister movie they're making or something. The usual codswallop. It was the only Twisted Sister song I could bear to sing! Which doesn't say much for their lyrical content… [We didn't record them both in] one take all together but it's one take of the backing track, one take for all the overdubs each.'

Another cover session the band would record with the production team of Bruce Boulliet and Bob Kulick was a cover of Metallica's 'Whiplash'. It was Motörhead's contribution to *Metallic Attack: The Ultimate Tribute*.

Bruce Boulliet engineered the session in its entirety, including the thrashing drum tracks. 'I was using the old silver 414s on the overheads, which is just a great mic for a situation where you've got a drummer like Mikkey, who's really hitting the drums and doing a lot of cymbal work. It's a solid mic that you don't have to worry about going out and they pick up enough high end that you didn't have to add much to the cymbal work but still keeps it a little bit gritty where it's rock'n'roll. On the snare, I used a 57 on the top and an AKG 451 on the underside and hat. 421 Sennheisers were on the toms. For the kick drum, I used a D12 inside and on the outside had it tunnelled off a little bit with some blankets with a Sound Deluxe U95 tube mic. I'd usually use ten to twelve tracks for Mikkey's drums, including a couple tracks for room mics – those were TLMs.'

Once he and Kulick turned their attention to guitar and bass overdubs, Boulliet explained, 'With Lemmy, generally, I found I was using a 421 and after I found out how Lemmy likes his bass to sound, added a 57 because he doesn't like a bunch of low. I shied away from a D12 or anything like that. For Phil's stack, I put up a couple 57s in front and maybe a 414 and combined it but, usually, just blended a couple 57s and everything ran through a couple Neve 1073 mic-pre's. I got on really well with Phil; I remember he came in with a six-pack of Mike's Hard Lemonade and we cut the tracks for the Metallica cover. He knew what he wanted and Lemmy would sit there, and he'd look to Lemmy for the solos and say, "How's that?" And sometimes Lemmy would say, "You've got better," so we'd keep whatever we thought was great and punch in from there.'

Vocally, the producer recalled, 'We'd use a U95 Sound Deluxe mic, which is a good all-around mic. Lemmy knew how to work the mic like a pro; he'd been doing it for so long all you had to do was set the mic up a little up above him and angled down, and he'd sing right up to it. It reminded me a lot of how you would see the old recordings back in the Capitol days when they would have the mic up and you would sing to it like that. I believe he just came from that school of recording and felt comfortable with it and incorporated that to his style. And he was Lemmy from the minute he would open his mouth, so you'd go, "There it is."

'You also had to remember that, when Lemmy was singing, you were going to get a healthy amount of cigarette smoke in your mic too, which to me is just part of rock'n'roll so I wasn't about to walk in the booth and say, "Listen, Lemmy, you can't smoke and sing in this mic..." I was the first one to walk in and put an ashtray in there for him and go, "That's good." He smokes while he sings and Lemmy doesn't like to be seen when he's recording, so we had to put up blankets over the windows and I just remember you could see over top the blanket a little bit and, while he was doing his vocals, you'd just see smoke coming out. I was cracking up. He was always solid doing his vocals – the guy by that point had sang on a million things and he was so on top of what he needed that rarely would you have to back and ask him, "Let's go back in and grab this word?" He already would say, "Right there, punch me in there," and knew where he needed to go. I never pushed to try and do too much of anything different from what he wanted. I would suggest some things and, if he didn't like it, just keep moving because he's obviously the artist and a legend, and invented a whole style, so I wanted to keep it as authentic as possible.'

That authenticity would earn the band their first ever Grammy award, for Best Metal Performance, reasserting their relevance to the metal genre as the millennium – and the band – continued to motor on.

Chapter Fourteen

Hammered: 2002

Lemmy – bass, vocals
Phil Campbell – guitar
Mikkey Dee – drums
Producers – Thom Panunzio, Chuck Reed and Lemmy
Engineers – Thom Panunzio, Chuck Reed and Bob Koszela
Released – 9 April 1992

Having survived 25-plus years in the business by the time of their 16th studio LP, *Hammered*, Lemmy told journalist Mark Carras he felt secure. 'We seem to be more or less of a fixture now. I'm not worried about our survival. I mean, our survival is guaranteed by the three members staying together.'

'It makes you feel good about the band,' he elaborated in interviews with journalists Claire Dyer and Scott Heller.

'Obviously we're doing the right thing... I am quite pleased with what we have done with Motörhead.'

Mikkey Dee talked with the band's biggest online fansite and journalist Marko Syrjala. 'Me and Phil write for five weeks, four weeks and we're finished,' he explained of the songwriting process. 'Usually, it's me and Phil who write most of the music, as you probably know, and Lemmy writes all his lyrics and then we piece it together... We write for ourselves and it's very spontaneous. We don't sit around and try to have a plan of what direction we want to go or anything, it's very spontaneous writing... We're all probably equal in deciding stuff, which is good because otherwise it wouldn't last... the fact that we write for ourselves makes it Motörhead...

'Me and Phil, we flew into LA on 10 September [2001] and we wrote these songs over the month of fuckin' fear over there, you know, it was a bad vibe. So maybe that had something to do with the mood of this album, I don't know. I was thinking about that afterwards. This album's actually really moody, you know? And the same goes for Lemmy, the way he wrote melodies...

'It seems to work for Motörhead, this way that we write the songs and, if we like it, we put it on the album. If we don't like it, we throw it out immediately. A lot of bands, they go in, they write songs and then six months later they go back and rearrange them, and then two months later they write another verse, you know. But it doesn't seem to work for Motörhead. Our albums are very spontaneous. What we feel today is what you get tomorrow, right there. What you hear tomorrow is not what we have felt for a year; this is what we feel right now. If we wrote an album today, just a few months later, it's going to be a completely different album and I think that's the only way of keeping Motörhead going forward. If we sit down and analyse what we're going to do, it's not going to be so true and I think you're gonna hear that in albums. You might get some songs that are more "Motörhead" for a lot of people but you're not going to get the honesty of the band.'

Adding insight into the latter, guitarist Phil Campbell, in an interview with the website www.live4metal.com, admitted, 'It gets a little harder to write songs we really like. We don't make any plans to do a fast album one year and a slow album the next… We never have any plans as such. It's a day-to-day thing with Motörhead.'

The band entered pre-production with producer Thom Panunzio, who points out the potential pitfalls in their creative approach. 'The band worked separately, a little more than I liked,' he explains, 'because Lemmy does the lyrics later. The band comes up with the music and then he comes up with the vocals after the fact. And I thought it would be better if everybody kind of worked together but it didn't work that way, so you have to adapt to the way they work. You take your track, you record it, then Lemmy works on it, gets the lyrics the way he feels their best, then comes in and you say, "Well, I think that's great, I think this line could be better," and he also changes it. He goes from one session to another revising the words, and just keeps improving and working to make the lyrics work better, rhyme better, to tell the story better. And Lemmy really, really worked hard at that, there's no question how hard these guys worked, it was just keeping them in cahoots with each other. Because, for instance, sometimes Lemmy would write lyrics later and we'd have to change something in the music to make it work with the way his lyrics worked. So that's the way we worked and made the record.

'So the record started in the rehearsal hall and I came down and they ran through a bunch of the songs for me, and I got familiar with the songs and, throughout rehearsals, they would tweak them now and then but, the more I was there hearing them, the more I could figure out arrangement and we did it together. The arrangements were really important to me: the song has to come first and then the arrangement has to be right to make it sonically great. If everything's clashing together, it doesn't work sonically. So with the song, you have to make sure you have the right verse and the transition into the bridge and the b-section, so at times I'd say, "This is a great verse but I don't think this chorus is great yet," or "The lead-up isn't strong enough," or whatever – and they were working on it at the same time. They had the music worked out but, again, a lot of times were playing it together for the first time, so there were things to figure out. So the pre-production was very important and is always to me – I usually won't go into the studio with a band until we go through the songs and have them worked out. Unless it's a Bruce Springsteen or U2-type situation where the artist writes in the studio, which is a different situation. It's more costly that way, so you have to work within the parameters of the band and, for Motörhead, they were really great in rehearsal – they rehearsed a lot and hard, and were used to doing it because they tour all the time, so doing pre-production before a record is like rehearsing to them. It is more difficult to do that in the rehearsal room than in the studio because you can't isolate the instruments and hear it as well and they play *really* loud, but that's the way we did it and it worked.'

When Thom Panunzio and drummer Mikkey Dee were ready to track drums, the producer recalls, 'We went into what was Henson Studios at the time –it used to be A&M, off Lebrea and Sunset here in Hollywood and, in the mid-1980s, Jimmy Iovine had been hired to rebuild those studios. And so Jimmy and his crew – which included me at the time – put those studios together. So I knew the rooms inside and out and there was one big room in the complex, Studio A, which was the biggest room and a very live room, and [it] had an old Neve console in it and was just perfect for recording drums in, so I suggested we go there and Mikkey loved the idea, and loved playing in the room. It's a great room for a rock drummer to play in because it's very live and he's such a hard-hitting, explosive drummer that it was the perfect environment for him. So we cut all the drum tracks in the big room and went for a really live, big sound and that room is one of the best rooms in the world to get that in – it sounds amazing. I produced and engineered the drum tracks and, on Mikkey's kit, we had a 57 in the kick, a Sennheiser shaver 421 in the kick and an RE20, an electro-voice mic, in the kick, then an 87 outside of the kick. And what I did was made a tunnel and blanketed it so the 87 wasn't actually in the kick itself. I always take the front head off, put the mics about halfway in and then usually always have an 87 outside of the drum but still covered up, so the sound isn't disbursing into the room. It's still being caught and still a tight sound. Then, on the snare, a 57 on the top and bottom, on the toms 421s just on the top, a KM84 AKG small pencil mic on the hi-hat and some 87s for overheads and 67s as room mics – probably three pairs up, so I had some 57s closer to the drums, then the 67s about halfway back in the room and then the 87s further back, picking up more of the room sound.'

Panunzio said, 'Mikkey was great – again, he's an unbelievable, hard-hitting, great drummer and we had the same vision on what the drums should sound like. We listened to other records he had made – Motörhead records – and wanted them to be big, live, explosive and wild. Mikkey tracked the drums on his own because he'd pretty much learned the songs before he went in and it is incredible; he just goes in and, without any guide tracks, does them live. He just sits there and goes, and is very well-rehearsed and has a great sense of keeping the tempo right, and knocks his parts out. It was pretty much in his head and he could go through those songs a couple of times and play it from top to bottom with no mistakes, which is pretty incredible with no one in there playing along with you, having anything to follow. There were times where he'd go back and say, "I could do that take better," and sometimes wouldn't even know what he was hearing and, a couple of times, I would hear a little flam here or there but, for the most part, he was right on. We went to tape, put it on two-inch multi-track analog tape and there might have been a little bit of editing later but nothing major. So basically, what he played is what you hear on the record. We knocked the drums out in two or three days. After we cut the basic tracks, we moved to Chuck's house.'

Co-producer Chuck Reed has a home studio to make any aspiring bedroom engineer jealous, including 'a Pro Tools system. The console was the Control 24 from DigiDesign and we had a really great front end on it. We used various microphones through Neve mic-pre's, all 1073s, and we used an 1176 and the LA2A, and Thom always brings his API lunchbox around. It's an EQ, so we had that there as well.'

Reed and Panunzio split production duties according to a long-established routine. 'Working with Thom for so long, we both came up with Jimmy Iovine and Thom had worked with Jimmy since the 1970s at the Record Plant in New York, so the band contacted Thom to produce the band, and he called me after he'd gotten the gig and brought me in to help out. Thom's not only a great producer but he's also an awesome engineer, but it's kind of tedious doing both at the same time, so I think my main help to him was engineering. We'd worked together for years and had gotten to know each other very well, so it was great working with him on that record. So after he'd done the drum tracking, my involvement in the studio freed him up to deal with the band more on the production side and oversee the engineering.

'In the course of producing the album, we didn't reference any specific previous Motörhead album, but rather the overall Motörhead vibe and feel. We wanted to capture the raw Motörhead sound you hear in the room as well as possible on tape. They play so powerfully as a live band, so I was trying to get really individually great sounds and then bring it all together like you're in the room with them, but as we recorded each member individually. Take the bass, for example. Lemmy's got his Rickenbacker through his crazy Marshall stack with the bass setting all the way off and everything else, settings-wise, all the way up and, if you go in the room while he's playing, you just feel that and we really wanted to make sure we captured that. We miked Lemmy with a U57 and an RE20 on his cabinet, and the different mics gave his sound different tonal quality, so it wasn't just the harshness of the 57. We were able to get some of the warmth out of the RE20 and I think we did have a Little Labs DI.'

On the recording of Lemmy's bass sound, shares Thom Panunzio, 'I realised after talking to him and getting to know him, he's never had a traditional bass sound and I didn't want him to have a traditional bass sound. I did try to encourage him to put a little more bottom in his bass and, when he explained that wasn't his sound, I had to respect that and still figure out how make a record that was sonically correct for the time because nobody wants to hear a bass with no bottom in it. So I had to figure out how to make a record that was sonically exciting and had the depth and the bottom that a record should have. So I didn't try to change his bass sound, which is more like another guitar – his bass is more in the mid-range than low-range frequency – so that's also a challenge because it clashes with Phil's guitar, since they're both somewhat in the same frequencies. Even though Phil's guitar is a little bit higher up in the spectrum, Lemmy's right up there. He plays a very bright, mid-rangy bass sound and he plays a lot of notes, so it took a lot of sitting at the board to get the guitar and the bass not to conflict with each other. To accomplish that, what I did was concentrated a lot more on the kick drum, especially for the bottom of the record. The miking also really mattered because I wanted to get the biggest, fullest sound and the most bottom I could get out of his sound without artificially adding it or asking him to change his EQ, so I had to make sure I had microphones that were giving me the full spectrum. I know I had a RE20 on the bass cabinet and an SM57 and 421 on it, wanting to make sure I was getting all the bottom that was coming out of there that was possible. You can boost the low end on an equaliser but, if it's not coming out of the instrument or the amp, it's not going to be any good. I probably spent more time miking his bass cabinet than I did miking anything else because I really wanted to make sure I was getting as much sound as possible out of it.'

Attention turned to Phil Campbell's guitar overdubs, as producer Panunzio explains. 'I would have ideas in pre-production on how I would map out the guitars and, first of all, they're all great musicians, they really are and Phil was an amazing guitar player… I've used him on sessions since after that record. He's got a style and a sound of his own. When you hear Phil play, you know it's Phil, just as when you hear Jeff Beck or Jimmy Page play, they have a sound, a characteristic to the way they play that you know its them. He's right up there with those guys, any of the great guitar players that play heavy music. And Phil can play a lot of different things, anything that has strings on it and, him being such a great guitar player, basically, I would just let him play. Of course, we'd work out the parts but there wasn't a lot of changes made in what he did, he's just that good. There were times where we'd double a rhythm guitar because we wanted the big stereo effect of two guitars and when the solo came in, you wanted them to pop out in the middle. So there were times we'd double things just to make it bigger but everything was driven by what the song called for. So I was just telling him things like, "Maybe let's double the rhythm," or "Let's just have one rhythm guitar and the lead played on the other side of the speaker," that's production, but I didn't tell him how to play. I might have said, "I like *this* solo better than *that* solo." Then there'd be days when he wanted to come in and make changes to a solo, or had different ideas, but he didn't play anything bad.

'Everything he played was well executed and it was really easy to get a good sound out of him. We did some experimenting and had a great relationship; he's a wonderful guy and one of the greatest guitar players I've worked with, seriously. So there wasn't a lot of ripping things apart, not a lot of editing. Occasionally he might want the end of one solo put on the beginning of another, or something like that, but it was pretty much what he played. I miked Phil with a 57 and a 421 right on the speakers and a 47 set back a bit from the cabinet, maybe a foot or two back, to pick up the whole sound.'

Elaborating on this aspect of the recording process, co-producer Chuck Reed recalled, 'We would, for the most part, go for the rhythms, then go back and do the leads. He did the rhythms all the way through for the most part, and we would double them as he played and then split them left and right. Phil was a great guitar player, he's does quick takes and, with his rhythms, he really had those locked down. His solos were really off the top of his head, so he might play one thing one day and then something entirely different the next day. We did a bit of comping on the leads because he'd play different solos all the time, so sometimes we would take the best parts of two or three solos and comp them together as one.'

As recording progressed into Lemmy's vocal sessions, Panunzio explained, 'We started doing vocals at Chuck's house. Lemmy does change his vocals as he goes along and so he would come over after the music was done to Chuck's studio to do vocals, and would show me the lyrics, go out and sing, and I might say, "This works, that doesn't," and a couple times I would say, "I think those lyrics are finished," then he would come back the next day with something new. He worked really, really hard and continued to work to improve his vocals, lyrics, background parts – everything – until he felt they were the best they could be.' Chuck Reed adds, 'We recorded Lemmy with a 57, except on "Serial Killer", which we used a really nice 251 tube mic on. That mic is very intimate vocal and in your face, as opposed to the full-out rock vocal style of the other songs. We'd always place the mic above his head, just like he sings live, and he did all his vocals in that same position. He's a great harmony singer; he'll go in and nail harmonies, and comes up right on the spot with great harmonies – it's really impressive. We got most of them done at my house but we were on a schedule so, by the time it was time to go in and mix, we had some vocal stuff we were still finishing and re-doing.'

To solve the problem, producer Thom Panunzio recalls they 'moved to a studio I'd set up on the fourth floor of the Interscope Office Building, on the A&R floor, and did most of Lemmy's vocals in Chuck's office at Interscope, which had a Pro Tools unit in it. We'd shut the air conditioners off, keep everybody out because it was a small room and had a live mic so we couldn't have anybody else in there anyway, and pretty much did all his vocals with just me and Chuck.

'Why we finished them at Interscope was, it came time to mix and Chuck's house wasn't set up for mixing and, because of my relationship with Interscope and the fact that I had put their studio together, Jimmy said, "You can use the studio to mix at." The band didn't have enough money at the time to go into a studio like this one to mix and I insisted on having a great room to mix in because I can't mix on shitty equipment in a shitty room. So we were allowed to come in at night and I mixed the record there, probably a hundred feet from Chuck's offices. There were times where I'd be in the studio mixing the rest of the album while we were still working on finalising Lemmy's vocal parts. So some nights I would just mix and others I'd come in and comp vocals with Chuck if that's what he was doing – it was an ongoing process. As Lemmy would change lyrics, or make something better, we'd replace maybe just a verse, or change a chorus, so most of the remaining lead-vocal tracking was done at Interscope.'

Chuck Reed: 'The Interscope studios at that time had one main studio and so we overdubbed in one of the offices because my office is actually a studio. So Thom would be in the mix room and we put Lemmy in one office and ran the mic lines into my office studio. My office studio had a full Pro Tools rig and outboard gear that included Neve mic-pre's, LA2As, 1176s, etc.'

'As a vocalist, I was impressed with the fact that Lemmy had such a good ear,' declares Panunzio. 'That did surprise me because he really has a musical ear and is really, really gifted. So it was really easy for him to sing a vocal, figure out a harmony part, then execute it right away, really easily. It was much easier than getting the lead vocals because the lead vocals involved the lyrics and other things. The backgrounds were a breeze – he would just whip those out in one or two takes. He sang in tune and wrote the parts, usually, right on the spot. "Thom, what do you think of this?" "Well, that might be too high. Why don't you try it lower?" So he'd drop it an octave or he'd say, "Let me put a high part on top of that." That's what surprised me the most, that he was almost like a studio session singer because you can have a rock band whose singer can stand at a mic for hours and hours and not get a vocal part right or in tune but a session singer can come in and knock it out in one or two takes, *boom*, *boom*, right on and they would do their parts real fast because they'd do jingles or commercials, all kinds of things. And probably the quickest and most professional musicians that came through the studio were background singers and Lemmy was just like one of them. It was just amazing, he was very gifted at that. He could sing the parts, come up with the parts, change them on the spot if I asked him to, and arranged them great in his head.'

Chuck Reed: 'Lemmy would write most of the lyrics during the recording sessions. I loved his lyrics and think Lemmy's underrated as a lyricist and his songs are deeper than just a hard-rock track.'

Attentions turned to mixing and Thom Panunzio 'didn't realise what a challenge it would be. Lemmy wasn't easy but

I wanted to do it – so we dove into it and did it. Why I knew it was going to be difficult was they're an intense band, they play a really hard, fast kind of rock and the harder, faster and more notes you play, the harder sonically it is to make it sound good. So my goal was to keep the Motörhead sound where I wasn't going to change their music and wasn't going to get them to play less notes or restructure what they did – because when I worked on songs with them, I wanted them to be Motörhead songs. They're a band that plays fast and hard so, again, it was difficult to hear all the notes and to have a clarity.

'If you have a track that's just kind of open, it's really easy to get the drums to sound great and if there's openness to it, there's room and you can hear things but that's not the style of their music. So it wasn't like, I want it to sound like this record or that record, I wanted it to sound like Motörhead – as vicious and intense as they were – but I insisted that, sonically, it was a record that, when it came on the radio or somebody dropped a CD in, it sounded like a record that was made in 2000, not the 1970s or 1980s. That was really my goal on the record and also to really push them to make their songs the best, which was also challenging to do. They write great songs, it's just challenging to push them to all work together and make the best of it. Just like any band, there's always challenges in pushing them to do their absolute best. I wasn't trying to reinvent them or get them to change their sound, or their music, or writing, but I wanted great songs that a lot of Motörhead fans would love and that would sound sonically great as a record. I thought that was very important for them and for their music to come across – especially these days with the technology we have. A lot of things sound better these days. It's not as difficult to make a band sound as good as they did back in the day when it was a lot more work. Nowadays, if the drum doesn't sound as good, you can sample it, or if a cymbal doesn't sound as good, you can auto-tune it, not that I did any of that with Motörhead but we kept it in mind. It also helped that we were mixing at Interscope, which had a full SSL 4072, a GE series.'

From a commercial point of view, the producer explained, they could relax in knowing that Motörhead weren't a Top 40 band. 'We didn't have to worry about getting a "single" mix really, so I did my best on every song and mixed the whole record pretty much the same way. The biggest challenge was to make the record have the full spectrum, being that it lacked that bottom from the bass guitar. Usually, the kick drum, in my opinion, if it's mixed right, is the lowest frequency so, if you look at the frequencies, its down in the lowest field somewhere around 50 and the bass guitar usually sits above that somewhere, maybe between 80 and 125, and also makes up the bottom of the record. So the challenge in mixing Motörhead was to have the record sound big and full without changing Lemmy's bass sound. Also, to keep the guitar and the bass so you could hear them without clashing with each other because, again, Lemmy plays the bass so much higher in frequency than most bassists that its up there in the guitar range. And you can only hear so many things in a range. So it was a challenge to get the guitar to be as present and as versatile as it is and still have the bass doing the same thing, because Lemmy's bass is really like another lead guitar – he plays so many notes that it's bright enough to be another guitar and that's what he's going for. To have those two things working together and not conflicting with each other, or obscuring each other, was one of my main focuses during mixing.' Chuck Reed adds, 'With mixing Lemmy's bass sound, we would try to warm it up as much as we could get away with, where Lemmy was still liking it, but we were able to keep some bottom, some punch in it.'

Panunzio worked to establish an atmosphere during the chaotic mixing sessions. 'I like having the band around during the mix,' he confirms, 'just for the vibe and the energy. Obviously, they don't need to be there in the earlier part of the day when we're getting the mix set up. Sometimes I would have Phil come in at the beginning of the mix so we could sort out his guitars and he was really helpful in helping me do that when there were choices to be made: "What guitar is better?" "Do we like this part with this part?" Sometimes we'd put down some options or, sometimes when it got to the mix stage, the double on a rhythm didn't sound as good as we first thought it did during tracking so I encouraged Phil to be around as often as he could – especially at the beginning of a session – so we could make sure that the guitars were all sorted out and that he was happy.

'Lemmy would usually come in later and listen and make comments, and he made good comments, but he wouldn't sit there and grind through it with me. He was also still working on vocals when I began mixing the record. I think Mikkey split and we sent him mixes to approve because, in the beginning after he'd finished tracking drums, I said to him, "Well, basically, this is what the drums are going to sound like," and I remember he was really happy with the drum sound.'

Chuck Reed's memories are mixed. 'It was a great experience,' he says, 'but there were definitely up days and not-as-up days, where some days something wouldn't be feeling right – and Lemmy can be very demanding in the studio – but, at the end of the day, he'd say, "All right, mate, see you tomorrow," and he lets it go. When he's at battle, he's definitely demanding but, once it's over, he's cool and wants to make sure people aren't going home angry. He just wanted to make sure we left with whatever it was worked out and that was only a few different times. Otherwise, the mixing process was pretty smooth sailing. I think the guys were very happy because it was sounding so good and I feel it was a great Motörhead album. I loved it, it sounds awesome, feels good, the songs are good. My favourites would have to be "Voices from the War", "Red Raw" and "Serial Killer" because, at the end of that song, his voice sounds almost like a wild animal, and I'd actually taken one of his breaths and ratted it out and used it at the end of the song, so... that animal-sounding breathing is actually his voice. I remember when I played that back for him and told him, "That's your voice on there, I used one of your breaths to make that sound," and he goes, "I know it's me fucking voice, I've been breathing most of my life." That was really funny – that's Lemmy.'

Released on 9 April 2002, in contrast to their last studio LP, *Rolling Stone* noted that the band's production team 'cleans up the Motörhead sound', while *Billboard* complimented the fact that, 'unlike many of the band's contemporaries, Motörhead manages to still release lean and mean rock records, while keeping the songs simple rather than adding some electronic accompaniment or trying to be current or hip.' In 'Walk a Crooked Mile', continued the magazine, 'Motörhead has written at least one more classic to add to the band's large number of hits, which could easily fill a double CD. Epic in length and with a cool bass line courtesy of Motörhead main dude Lemmy Kilmister, "Walk a Crooked Mile" has a bit of a punk edge to it, like a lot of Motörhead's tunes, but it also closes with a stylish 1980s-style metal guitar solo. The rest of the material does not veer from the usual Motörhead formula... it's all played dirty and in the gutter, and will undoubtedly appeal to Motörhead's dedicated fan base.'

In interview with www.rockezine.com, Mikkey Dee

revealed, 'When we first wrote these songs I thought they were going to be super-good. And then when we started recording it, let's say halfway through this album, I thought, this is going to be the worst shit album we've ever done. The songs didn't come out the way you saw it. But then, in the end, it all turned again and they turned out to be actually pretty good... This album would have sounded very different if we'd recorded it next year, you know? This time, things were kind of moody. We entered the studio on 10 September, the day before the terrorists' attacks at the WTC. Of course these events influenced us in how we were feeling while recording *Hammered*... It's more melodic. And it's darker and it's bluesier, rockier because we are more that way than before... But this one takes a little more listening and I think it's going to last a little longer, maybe... I think this one is going to grow to something like that. But it's not an immediate album, no. Why? I don't know.'

For his own part, producer Thom Panunzio was pleased. 'When we were done I was very happy and very proud of the record. At times it was difficult working with Lemmy, at times he can be really tough. He gave me a run for my money, I've got to say, and I've worked with some tough guys. I think, to be honest, at that point in my career someone could rile me, or get to me, and Lemmy definitely did and we had our moments, a couple of times when we would clash. But what was the most rewarding thing for me at the end of the day, I was very proud of the record and very happy with the way it came out, and really happy that I was able to deliver a record that was sonically great, and that Lemmy was happy.

'Near the end of mixing, he'd always be drawing or doing something and I remember on the last day – Lemmy being a tough guy, pretty hard, doesn't say "thank you" much, he's not emotional – he was doing some drawing and, when he was all done, he handed me and Chuck each a drawing he'd done, which had on it a code of arms with our initials in it, like a plaque and each of ours were different. He also drew this cartoon with this caption that said, "Thanks for getting the popcorn out of the bear trap." He knew how difficult he could be and how tough it was at times.

'There were nights that I walked out of those sessions and needed a drink, where he would give me a hard time – there's no other way to say it – and he knew that, and appreciated that I stuck in there and made a great record for him. That's what he meant by that "thanks for getting the popcorn out of the bear trap". In the end, it was all well worth it and I'm glad I did it, and would do it again in a second. By the time I worked with them, I'd done a lot a lot of work with a lot of famous people but to have Motörhead on your resume, no matter what other records I'd made, I'd always want to have that. So that's why I did it, because of the history of the band, their music: it was a challenge. I knew it would be and it wasn't something I did for money but, again, it's always great to be associated with a band like that, especially in my world. And Motörhead is a band I'd want to be associated with — whether they sell one record or a million records. They're icons and I was proud to have my name on the record as producer. It's great to say I produced this guy and this guy and Motörhead — it's not something everybody can do.'

Chapter Fifteen

Inferno: 2004

Lemmy – bass, vocals, harmonica
Phil Campbell – guitar
Mikkey Dee – drums
Producing, mixing and engineering – Cameron Webb
Released – 22 June 2004

In 2004, Motörhead began to experience a sonic renaissance of sorts, hooking up with in-demand metal producer Cameron Webb. 'My working with Motörhead first came about through a meeting with their manager Todd Singerman and he'd used me for other records for other bands for a couple years. I think he was testing me out a little bit because I always used to say to him, "Let me have a shot at the next Motörhead record," and he'd always laugh at me and say, "No, no, I'd never put you through that." And then it came up where Lemmy wanted to do a new record, so Todd called me and said, "Hey, you have a chance to work on the new record but here's what we have to do: we have to meet at the Sunset Marquis [hotel] and sit down and talk with the band and, if they like you, you've got the record, if they don't like you, forget it.

'So we sat down, had a steak dinner and just talked about what the direction of the record should be. And I think the band trusted Todd because of my past records with him, so we just discussed things and I probably made a couple mistakes with things I said during the conversation but I also work really hard and have listened to them for years – one of my favourite records by Motörhead is *Rock'n'Roll*, which has "Eat the Rich" on it. I used to listen to that in high school when I first got introduced to Motörhead.

'One mistake I'd made at that first meeting was that I told the band I liked Motörhead as a really heavy group and Lemmy looked at the band as more of a rock'n'roll group. Because I'd told them at the meeting, "I want to make this record super-heavy." I don't wanna say compared to a Slayer record because it's not that heavy but it has those elements of the System of a Down records, with really heavy, heavy tones and a really thick, thick wall of everything, as opposed to a trashier sort of sound. I liked the slickness of that and, when I said I wanted to make a heavier record, instantly Lemmy said, "Well, I make rock'n'roll records, I don't make heavy records."' Lemmy himself explains, 'I liked the old stuff – The Beatles, the old Stones, all kinds of shit, Little

Richard, so I consider myself to be in a rock'n'roll band.' But nevertheless, Webb recalls wondering whether he'd made a fatal mistake in his comment at that all-important meeting. 'Fuck, I just screwed up... So when we left the meeting Todd said, "You only made one mistake in the whole conversation – it was that damn rock'n'roll comment you said because Lemmy likes rock'n'roll, not that heavy stuff." And I replied, "Well, that's what I want to do for them, we'll see what happens." So we got on that first day and started pre-production like a week later.'

Webb quickly learned that working with the band would be a true departure from any norms he'd previously held to in the course of producing. 'Pre-production on the first record was most unique because I didn't know how Motörhead worked. So what happened was we went up to a rehearsal studio across the street from NRG [recording studios] and the band was in a big rehearsal room, and I walked in and said, "Hey guys, I want to hear some of the songs, play me some songs." So Mikkey and Phil walked up on the stage, got their instruments and Lemmy walked into another room with the doors open. And I asked, "Where's Lemmy going? I thought we were going to run through some songs?" And Phil said, "Lemmy doesn't play songs, he's going to write lyrics while we're rehearsing the songs." And I was kind of blown away and asked, "Well, will he play bass for me?" And they said, "No, he's not going to do that because he's writing lyrics."'

In an interview with www.rockezine.com, Mikkey Dee

explained the truly serendipitous creative process. 'Most of the songs are composed in their rough versions by Phil and myself. Later on, Lemmy comes in and writes the melodies and lyrics. A Motörhead album is composed in a very spontaneous way, which means it all depends on the moment and the feeling we have at that particular moment in time.'

Guitarist Phil Campbell told www.live4metal.com and journalist Gary James, 'We don't have a life plan or nothing, it's just the way the songs come out at the time… We don't write anything on the road really. We just set aside a certain time to write, go into a rehearsal room and just bang the songs off. When we're on the road we don't write. We'd rather drink instead. We'd like to do it pretty quickly when we do have to write songs.'

Lemmy, for his own part, confirmed the band's down-to-earth attitude. 'Mostly, we get the song first and then put the words on top of it. I like to have silence when I'm writing lyrics but can be in a room of people – I just tell them all to shut up.' Of his lyric-writing process, Lemmy told journalist Mark Carras and the *Columbus Dispatch*, 'When I sit down to write, things appear. It's really weird, things appear under my pen and I have no idea where they come from, you know? It's just having a good vocabulary and letting your mind open up and translate it… We write about five weeks before the initial recording. We write the bare bones of the music and bring them into the studio and work the lyrics out there.'

Webb remembers witnessing Lemmy in full creative flow on occasion. 'On that first record, throughout all the pre-production, I'd walk in and he'd be writing lyrics while the band was rehearsing, and show me lyrics and we'd talk about stuff but, generally, Mikkey and Phil would work out all the parts and they'd all approve it, and I would make suggestions. "Try this fill here, or double-time here." It's like this with every artist, until they become your friend and before you can trust each other: they have to be careful with me and I have to be careful with what I say. So I would say what I had to say and sometimes they would turn it down and other times they would say, "Hey, that's a great idea, let's move this around or do that." This came up more so with arrangements. At that rehearsal studio, everything was miked up anyway so they would burn me CDs to take home and listen to as well.'

The songs developed and Webb began to map out a sonic blueprint for their direction. 'Two important things I wanted do to differently from past records with the new album,' he recalls. 'First, my whole direction was to be slick and produced and big, and the thing about Motörhead was, over a period of time, there'd been records that were trashier and then records that were super, super-slick, so they'd kind of rounded the whole spectrum of everything. And the last couple Motörhead records were a little trashier sounding, where I was more a fan of the records Howard Benson had made with them – they were killer and really, really big sounding and huge. And again, with the last couple of albums they'd made before I worked with them, I felt things had gotten a little out of control, and I wanted to control that again and put it in a package where it was heavy and big and you could turn it up loud and it sounded great, and to be comparable with a new System of a Down or Slayer record, more like bands that were newer and had a fresher sort of sound. Even Soundgarden – those big, big sounds. With Motörhead I wanted to keep the band progressing as they went on.

'One thing I learned really quickly as we got into pre-production is Motörhead doesn't do anything that they don't want to do. So if I would have come to them and said, "I'm going to make you sound like this," they would have told me to fuck off, so you don't do that. Basically, you kind of give them a direction and have to gain their trust and then show them. "Lemmy, can we try an extra harmony?" and, "I love what you used to do in this way on your old records. Why aren't you doing that now?" You have to introduce it so that you're not saying, "This is what you're going to do." So because Motörhead does what they want to do, I had to find ways to suggest new things to them and reign that into a record.'

The band entered the studio to begin recording their 17th studio LP and Webb recalled, 'We tracked drums at NRG Studios in Studio A, which had an old vintage-series Neve console and has a really nice drum room. Mikkey has a big kit and, in general, has the same set-up – same amount of toms and double kick drums where he played with two pedals. On the first album I remember I miked the kick drums with Audio-Technica ATM25s inside the kick and then there's these outside sub-kick drum mics that kind of look like a little drum — Yamaha makes them — and I used a pair of those on the outside kick. Every tom was miked and, for overheads, normally I would do stereo but, with Mikkey, instead of two overheads I would do three overheads and mic the ride and the hat by themselves. And those overhead mics would have been AKG C12s. For the snare, I miked with a 57, which I pretty much used for every record.'

Mikkey Dee provided drums which were near perfect and which should have been straightforward to track but the producer explains, 'The first record was really difficult to record because, first off, it didn't help that I was a lot younger than them. They looked at me and didn't know who I was because, in a way, to them I was this stranger walking into their musical world, asking them to change things and do things. So I remember on the first record we were sitting in NRG and had had a drum tech in the morning and the drums sounded awesome, and Mikkey did his first drum take of the first song on the album, hits the last snare. And I hit the talkback and say, "Hey, Mikkey, can we do that one more time?"

'He was already walking into the control room by that time and sits down next to me at the console and says, "OK, what's the next song? Let's go." And I go, "We didn't finish this one yet," and he says, "What do you mean, dude? That take was freaking perfect!" And everyone's in the room and I'm this young guy and they don't know me very well, and I'm like, "No, that's not perfect. I can probably point out seven to twelve mistakes," and he looks at me and goes, "Prove it right now!" So I kind of smiled and said, "I'm going to hit this button right here every time there's a mistake and it's going to put a yellow marker on the screen, so let's listen to the song and see how many we get to." So he goes, "Fine, go for it," and I start the song and hit the button – *one*, *two* – and by the time I get to seven he goes, "Turn that fucking thing off! I'm going to go in and do it again," and stormed out of the room. And Phil and Lemmy were pretty quiet but kind of laughed because they knew I was right. And it was hard to stand up to Mikkey, knowing how good a drummer he was.'

But the pair eventually reached an accord. 'We tracked drums over three days at NRG,' says Webb, 'and Phil would lay down a scratch track with Mikkey playing and Lemmy in the control room. They were all there but he wasn't playing. It went that way with all three records; we'd do drums then go back and record everything else. Mikkey left pretty much a couple days after we finished drums and then came back for the mix. Then we moved over to Paramount Studios and did the rest of the record on an SSL console, and also mixed it at Paramount Studios on an SSL 9000. So we got to work on the three nicest consoles you can use.'

In contrast to past studio experiences where he'd seemed most interested in getting through the recording process as quickly as possible, Lemmy now seemed more prepared to get into the technical side of things. 'I like the studio a lot more now than I used to,' he says. 'I've gotten to know the studio a bit better and can talk that language a bit better. I don't mind Pro Tools, I don't have a problem as long as it sounds good to us. That's what we're doing – if you like it too, it's a bonus! It's the same with working live off the floor: sometimes it works better and sometimes not. In the old days you had to but we over-dubbed more on the later albums.'

Sooner or later Webb had to be initiated into recording Lemmy's bass. 'When you deal with an artist who's done twenty records and has worked with a lot of producers, you try to prove yourself that you're more prepared in the whole process,' he explains. 'So for me, what I would do is get the gear there a day early and would set up, knowing Lemmy's tone and what it was from rehearsals and how he was going to tweak his amp. He basically had a normal Marshall cabinet, as well as this special Marshall cab, that had 415s in them – so there were two main speaker cabs that you were working with. Then he had a couple Super Bass 100 amps he's been playing for his whole career, so the Marshall's the main one and then another that's a little different. So I would use a 57 on the normal Marshall cabinet and then use a Fet 47 on the bigger one. What I would do in addition to all that was also run another amp – because, if you listen to Lemmy's tone, his knobs, the way he does it is turn the bass to zero, the mids to ten, and the treble and presence he kind of puts in the middle. So if you think about it, there's no bass and he's the bass player.'

Continuing, Webb explained, 'When I ran that second amp, I'd run it through like a fifteen-inch speaker and run it separately and totally out of it, so I would get a deeper sort of tone. But here's the key because Lemmy doesn't want bass, he wants his bass to sound like guitar. So what I would do is record that but I would mute it and I treated it more like a safety so, when I was mixing, if I needed more bottom end, I would bring that up. And if Lemmy didn't like the tone, he would yell at me and say, "Hey, what did you do, put that low bass tone in there? Get that shit out of there!" And he'd swear at me and I'd turn it off and let it sit, and on the first record he didn't notice it as much but on the second and third albums, *Kiss of Death* and *Motörizer*, he was tearing me apart whenever he was hearing, in a sense, too much bottom end on the bass. I had to do that sort of thing on each record but in different ways because on the first record I didn't know what to expect. So I gave him a bass tone when I first plugged in the tone and he said, "Man, that sucks. What are you doing?" And then he tweaked his amp and all of a sudden my tone was fucked. So I basically had to adapt and get that other amp set up and organised but do it in kind of a sneaky fashion because he didn't want that on his bass tone. But I had to make sure I was safe later on in mixing in case Mikkey or Phil said, "Hey, where's the bottom end?" So miking Lemmy's bass, in general, was complicated to set up because I would use at least two amps and at least three cabinets on everything, then get his tone exactly the way he wanted it and then get another one for mixing with that second cabinet. He also recorded DI and Lemmy doesn't like hearing the sound so that would usually be muted and, if I even used the DI I, would have to distort it to make it sound any good. Lemmy played a Rickenbacker, that's what he always liked to use.'

The producer's attention turned to tracking the guitar sound and Webb revealed that – as challenging as drum tracking with Mikkey had proved on certain levels – where working with Phil Campbell was concerned, the challenges rose to a whole new level. 'It's day one, I'm supposed to start guitars with Phil and bring him down to this place in Orange County called Maple Studios, which is about forty-five minutes from LA, and he leaves at 3.30pm and hit traffic, so he didn't get down to me till about 7pm. It was a summer day, hot as hell, his car didn't have air conditioning, so he came in as grumpy as you could ever imagine and didn't want to be there at all. So we ended up doing guitars that day but didn't finish the song we were working on, then he came back the next day amid the same problem with traffic and it just didn't work. And at the end of that day, he goes, "You're fired! I don't want to do guitars with you, we're done. I don't even want to see you again." So I called the manager and he said, "You're not fired, Cameron, Phil's just being crazy. We'll figure it out." Well, what I'd found out that had really happened was that Phil wanted to do guitars with one of his friends and didn't want to work with me, so this was a good excuse for him to get rid of me.'

Continuing, the producer explained, 'What we did was work out a deal where Phil tracked the guitars at someone else's studio and the plan was that I would go to LA and do bass with Lemmy when they'd finished. Well, the problem was that two weeks later I get all the guitar tracks and I didn't like any of them. I didn't like the tone, I had tuning issues with all of them and didn't like the tightness of them. So basically, I told the manager, "I need Phil to come in and re-do all of these guitar tracks," and he didn't want to do it because, obviously, he had just done all the guitars. But the guitars weren't up to my standard at all, so we had a big blow out and, in the end, Phil ended up coming in just to do a couple of songs over.

'For Phil's guitar sound on the first two records we used JCM900 Marshall cabinets with a 57 and 421 on the cab and I was really stoked on those; I thought they sounded great. At first we'd tried combining amps but found it sounded best with just the one head and one or two cabs, and then I would double the guitars. So as each day would go by, I'd do a song a day with him and then do bass with Lemmy after that. And each day, as Phil finished retracking his guitars, I'd say, "OK, cool, that one's done. What's the other song?" And he would say, "No, no, I'm only doing one song," so each day for eleven days, we would do one song of guitars. And he knew what I was doing; he knew I was trying to replace all the guitars on the record so, when we got to the last song, he looked at me and said, "I'm not doing this one, I've already done this twice, there's no way I wanna do this again." So here's the funny thing: that one song was the first song we'd done at Maple Studios that day when he fired me, so I actually ended up using those tracks. He probably knew that but at the moment, was upset at me because I was making him re-do everything. I didn't realise, at first, that Phil would be disappointed by doing that process. That's why it was more of a mistake than anything because we were figuring each other out.'

That process extended itself as well to vocal tracking, with producer Cameron Webb recalling that 'the very first time I recorded Lemmy, it was similar to the Mikkey thing, where Lemmy had never sung the song before but he'd sung it in his head and obviously had written it on paper, and he went in the booth, sang it once and was then, "Ah, let me have another take." So he sang it a second time and, by the time he came back into the control room, I had comped a couple of lines from one take to the other take and he was like, "OK, I want to hear the second take," so I had comped it all onto the second take. So when I played him the second take, he spotted the three spots where I'd put the other line in – same melody, just with a better performance – and he kind of caught me right there and said, "Hey, don't mess with my vocals. I sang that because I wanted to fucking hear that, so give it back to me." So I gave him back that but what I learned with that is there's no mic check, there was literally him walking into the room and singing. If I hadn't had my levels right, I would have been in so much trouble and would have lost those two takes that were really important.

'So looking at that process of how he builds a track, he's good and he's been doing it so long that he knows how do melodies and harmonies, and when you actually do the harmonies with him, he'll come up with ideas and do one harmony, then say, "That's pretty cool, let me do a harmony on top of that one," and then he'll add a third and a fourth one, and sometimes they're more monotone and sometimes they move a lot, it just depends.' Lemmy adds, 'With vocals now, they're a lot more involved... compared to the first records.'

The producer came to discover that, despite appearances, 'Lemmy is a very sensitive person and on the first album he had a girlfriend at the time, so he was very inspired when he was writing his lyrics and singing them. I always use Neve mic-pre's for Lemmy's voice and a Neumann U67 on his vocals. Harmonies are interesting with Lemmy because I think, if you listen back to those records he did with Bill Laswell in the 1980s, *Orgasmatron* and *Rock'n'Roll*, there's a lot of harmonies on those records, which established a certain sound that, when you heard those kind of harmonies, you went, "Fuck, that's gotta be Motörhead." So when I came into this record, I was pushing for that a little because, if you just listen to Lemmy's lead vocal with nothing else up, you go, "Oh, that's Lemmy," but when you put those harmonies he does in there, then you go "Woah, that's Motörhead!" So whenever Lemmy said, "I want to do a harmony," I would say, "Let's go, let's do it!" I always embraced any sort of element of what he wanted to do – vocally or otherwise – but especially where harmonies were concerned because I knew how important it was to Motörhead's signature sound. So in general, when he had a harmony idea, I would just let him have at it and, if I had an idea, I would also say, "Lem, I want a harmony here," and he would give me some great, whacked-out harmony. The funny thing about Lemmy is – because he has a rock voice – people are always saying, "Oh, he's probably not a good singer" when, actually, he's an *amazing* singer and he's great at writing harmonies.' In terms of specific highlights, Webb cites the recording of what would become the album's first single, 'Whorehouse Blues', 'which I love because, when he sang it to me, I felt like it was that Lemmy voice that people never hear because he sang like that before, but never on bigger songs, I don't think. So to me, it was kind of touching to hear his voice like that because it was real. I was always really proud of that song because it was a different element.'

Once production had wrapped, Webb's focus shifted to mixing. 'The best part was Mikkey flew back into town and he, Phil and Lemmy were all there at Paramount. What happened was, I'd get there early in the morning, work until three or four in the afternoon when the band would show up, and I'd play them the mix I'd been working on and Mikkey would tell me to turn up the drums, turn up the snare, Phil would tell me to turn up the guitars, Lemmy would tell me to turn up the bass and, when I did that, everything was distorted, everything sounded bad, so then they'd ask me to go back to the way it was. So I'd do that and then what would happen was I got them fighting against each other, which was actually of benefit for me because I could get them to team up against each other, which is a good and bad thing. In general, Lemmy always wanted to hear the bass really loud and would say, "I wanna hear the fuckin' bass," and how loud he wanted it would muddy up everything else, unfortunately. So when I would turn it that loud, Phil and Mikkey would say, "Hey, now I can't hear snare, or the guitars," so we argued a lot back and forth, and ended up compromising a lot on that first record, which is why, personally, I like the sound of that record best because I feel like it was a little more controlled and didn't get as out of control because of that element of compromise.'

The album was released on 22 June 2004 and *Rolling Stone* hailed the band's new studio LP as a triumphant return 'back-to-brutal-basics, riffing like a rocket-fuelled Chuck Berry: no mercy, no quarter, no prisoners... *Inferno* blazes ahead with the same full-bodied attack as on their early classics, keeping their big-ass riffs, speed-punk grooves and Lemmy's doomsaying bullshit free.' *Billboard* celebrated the fact that, 'like AC/DC, Motörhead rarely stray from their niche, crafting reliable records from a punk-metal template that began in 1977 with their self-titled debut. *Inferno* is no exception, as the sum of its parts does little to deviate from the formula. Opening with the blistering "Terminal Show" – marking the first of two appearances by guitar legend Steve Vai – Lemmy, Philip and Mikkey burn through twelve raucous, blues-rock fist-pumpers with the energy of a trio of wily twenty-somethings. Lemmy's gruff vocal style is ageless.'

Cameron Webb's proudest moment in the course of making his first album with Motörhead came 'after the first record – Lemmy called me up and said, "I've never done this before, called a producer and said thank you," and I said, "Why?" and he said, "Because you trusted in me and believed in me."

'I've never been through so much emotional drama on records than I have on Motörhead records because I'd go home some nights saying to myself, I don't know if I want to go back tomorrow because they were very difficult records to make. Two of the guys are British, so their humor was different than mine and they speak what they want, and if they don't like something or don't think it's good, they'll call it a piece of shit. Rather than saying, "Hey, that's not good," they'll say, "That's the worst thing I've ever fucking heard in my life," and it's just their English humour – which is very difficult sometimes for this American to deal with, I would say.

'I'm really proud of that record. I put a lot of effort into it and, sometimes when people comment about records,

"This could have been better, or that could have been better," that kind of comment to me – when I do Motörhead records – I say, "You know what? If you could sit in this chair for one fucking day, you'd walk out of here and quit." Unless you're actually sitting there and seeing the process through, you don't know what can actually happen. We had a lot of hard times and a lot of fun times – higher highs and lowers lows with doing Motörhead than any other band I've worked with. So for me, I'm really proud of the records we've made together.'

Lemmy expressed his feeling in his autobiography that, with *Inferno*'s release, 'we've been making the best records of our career', further adding in an interview at the time with *Rolling Stone*, 'I think by this time we should have our own category: Motörhead music.'

Chapter Sixteen

Kiss of Death: 2006

Lemmy – bass, vocals, sketches, handwriting
Phil Campbell – guitar, backing vocals
Mikkey Dee – drums
Producing, mixing and engineering – Cameron Webb
Released – 29 August 2006

Diving into his second collaboration with Motörhead on 2006's *Kiss of Death*, recalls producer Cameron Webb, was a contrast to their first outing together in the studio. Pre-production was 'a little easier because the band understood what I did when I walked in the door. They would give me the instrumentals and I would say, "Hey, I love all this but don't understand this one part, this other part could be your chorus, or this could be your verse," and they might say, "No, you're right," or Lemmy might say," "No, you're wrong,' it just depended on the situation. I'd learned a lot about them and to respect them more than I had before as people, and in terms of what they liked to do, so I let them be more rock'n'roll – in a sense – on that second record because that's what I knew they wanted to be. But I didn't want anything to be sloppy or messy, but when they were writing and recording the songs, I went for more of that rock'n'roll edge, more what Lemmy and Motörhead want to be versus what Cameron wants to shape Motörhead to be, in a sense. As they knew me better, it was kind of easier.'

For Lemmy, the process of making records never got old even as he himself approached his 60s, as he told the *Independent*. 'You wouldn't say Beethoven was past it, would you? The Beatles are the classical music of rock'n'roll. And rock'n'roll is far more widespread than classical will ever be. So I don't see why there should be a point where everyone decides you're too old. I'm not too old and until I decide I'm too old I'll never be too fucking old.' In the same interview, Kilmister revealed that the band's writing process remained as spontaneous as ever. 'We do not plan things,' he declared. 'It's like I always figure, if you make plans, they usually fuck up, you know? If you just go in like under the knife, you usually come up with something decent.'

In an interview with www.ultimate-guitar.com, Campbell explained that 'we write songs for the three of us, we don't write them for anyone else, we don't write for people who buy the records. I know it's a strange thing to say but we don't write for people who buy 'em 'cause we write what we want to write for the three of us. And that's sort of what's kept us going... Once you start writing with other people in mind, if you're a band in our situation, for Motörhead, it is like a kiss of death, actually. 'Cause the purity is gonna go out of there.'

Cameron Webb: '...when they chose me to do the second record... I asked Lemmy, "How come you chose me to do the second record?" He said, "You know what? Because you'll stand up to any of us – me, Phil, Mikkey – and not many people will do that.' Because people are afraid of the star factor with bands like that and that first day Lemmy goes, "You gained a lot of respect because you sat Mikkey down and told him he was not as perfect as he thought he was, and you made him play better and play great on that record." And I really listened to every hit and every fill and really paid attention, and where I thought he could do better, I would ask him to do better – even when he didn't want to. I would push him as far as I could because I know how good Mikkey is and that sometimes, if someone pushes him, he can do even better, and I think I helped him achieve that and hope he's proud of those records.

'On *KOD*, we tracked drums at NRG and, with Mikkey, basically, Lemmy trusted me with the drums in general and Mikkey's an insane drummer – he's one of the best in the world, so he's not making mistakes, really. He's a good drummer, he knows where the pockets are so you could put a monkey behind the boards with Mikkey and get an amazing drum record. On *Kiss of Death* and *Motörizer*, I used

Fet 47s on the outside kick and, again, Audio-Technica ATM25s inside the kick and the 57 on the snare.'

Once drums had been tracked, the producer recalls, the band decamped and 'recorded the rest of the record at Paramount Studios'.

Lemmy recalls his bass included the traditional line-up of 'Marshall stacks, Killer and Murder One – they're both just great old amps that were vintage. An amp changes as it gets older and you have to rewind the output transformer sometimes and replace valves – some valves are better than others.' But this time his producer had a better idea of how to tackle the set-up. 'By the second record, I knew what Lemmy wanted more in his bass sound and I'd wanted a certain thing on the first record and was trying to work together with Lemmy to get that, and by the second record, I knew in a sense what he wanted, so I shot more for that in his initial tone right away. It's hard because that amp, when you turn it that way, the way it distorts is kind of uneven sometimes, so you have to crank everything really loud to make it really push and keep everything pumping really well. So I wouldn't say I did things different – I miked things the same – but I knew what he wanted earlier on in the process, so I was able, I think, to achieve it much faster.'

He had also discovered the key to tracking both Lemmy and Phil Campbell. 'Not taking Phil out of his element; he needed to be in Hollywood,' confirms the producer. 'He and Lemmy both needed to be close to where they were staying and Phil lives in Oakwood, so he could drive right over the hill to the studio and Lemmy was in West Hollywood, so I found a studio that was close by. I just needed to cater to them more. On the first record, while it was tough in the beginning, once we got a guitar track, Phil was good. On the second record, he knew he was going to have to do guitars and double guitars, so when he came in he was a little easier to work with, I would say, and we had the same basic amp and miking set-up, so the second album was definitely the easiest to do.'

In his www.ultimate-guitar.com interview, Campbell said, 'I listen to a lot of stuff but when I come up with something, it's purely Motörhead in mind, you know? It's pointless to listen to something that somebody else has done… When I first started, I'd play a guitar solo in the studio and I'd say, "Well, what do you think of that, boys?" and somebody'd say, "Ah, that's brilliant," and somebody would say, "That's the worst thing I've ever heard in my life." And you'd be there thinking, well, is it brilliant or is it crap? And things will get confused. You might change one bit and leave another bit, and things get watered down and the purity goes… So we just write what we feel is good at the time.'

Webb noticed that the songwriting process remained largely unchanged. 'On the second record, Lemmy did some writing in pre-production but he also did a lot of writing in the studio as we were tracking. That was the biggest shock for me because, basically, he would sit there and write a song, and then go into the booth and sing it.

Here's what would happen: if he would sing the song one time and I didn't say anything after the take, he would normally know I was starting to think and about to make a suggestion, and he would just walk back in the control room, and sometimes, if he agreed with me, he'd just start rewriting the song right there. He'd go sit in the front of the room, rewrite, spend a half-hour, then walk back in the booth and say, "OK, I want to sing it again," and he'd have a completely different song – new melodies, new lyrics – and then we'd go sing that song. So while some of that pre-production writing was used, a lot of it wasn't because he probably wrote, on average, twenty songs in pre-production and then another twenty-five to thirty during recording in the studio through the rewrites. On the second record there was a *lot* more writing in the studio than on the first record. Lemmy had a girlfriend on the second record, so he was also very inspired. There's a song called "God is Never on Your Side" from *Kiss of Death*, which I think is amazing, and a song called "Christine", which was written about Lemmy's girlfriend at the time, and I love that song too.'

From a technical vantage point, the producer felt that 'tracking Lemmy's vocals was easier on the first two records because the vocal booth at Paramount is a small room and I'd seen footage of Motörhead live and had seen them live myself many times before working with them, so I knew you had to point the mic down and he would lean up, so I knew initially that was how I was going to set it up.

So I set him up with a U67 and that worked great. As with the first album, when it came time for harmonies, Lemmy would have done his lead vocal and then gone into his harmony-building process, same as the first album.'

As he tracked Lemmy's vocals, Webb revealed that, even as he produced the track, he was always thinking of the mixing stage at the same time. 'I track in the mindset of "how am I going to mix this record?" So if I'm asking Phil to add a bunch of guitars, I'm not just adding them to add them, I'm adding them because I know I'm going to want the chorus to jump up or I know I want a lead part to go here. So in the back of my mind, with Motörhead or any other band, when I'm tracking I'm also mixing. Now, when I mix, I start from scratch, everything gets dropped down and I re-do absolutely everything but I'm always very conscious of what the end product is going to be – I'm always listening thinking, OK, this song's great but why doesn't this outro punch? Or maybe it needs a harmony, or maybe needs another background here, or a distorted vocal? So when I mix, it's always about thinking what the final stage is going to be, that's the key.'

Once mixing got underway, the producer immediately noticed some differences to the way it had gone down before. 'Lemmy and Phil were in the studio but Mikkey was in Sweden. On the second and third albums I would send him emails with songs in progress and, if he didn't like vocals or lyrics, we'd discuss it back and forth. So when I would finish a mix, I would send it to Mikkey and it would take a day or two's response to get his notes back. Well, he always thought the snare was flat and Lemmy was always trying to push the bass up too loud, so that record was difficult to mix and, I would say, not as polished as *Inferno* because I didn't have them all in one place while the mix was happening.'

Upon release on 29 August 2006, *Kiss of Death*'s impressive worldwide chart debuts reflected the band's sustained popularity with one of metal's fiercely loyal fan bases. It debuted at UK No. 45 and did well all over Europe. Critics seemed most impressed that on the album the band 'still sound very much like Motörhead', as www.mtv.com noted, while *Billboard* highlighted the fact that 'in the metal community there are two veteran/legendary bands that, whenever they release a new album, you know pretty much what you're going to get. We're talkin' 'bout AC/DC and Motörhead, of course… *Kiss of Death* easily manages to slay most of the fly-by-night foolers that are currently being showcased on the airwaves.'

Chapter Seventeen

Motörizer: 2008

Lemmy – bass, vocals
Phil Campbell – guitar
Mikkey Dee – drums
Producing, mixing and engineering – Cameron Webb
Released – 26 August 2008
Peak Chart Position: UK No. 32; US Top 200 No. 82

By the time 2008's *Motörizer* roared on to the metal scene, Motörhead's status as the godfathers of speed metal had been firmly established, as *Billboard* reflected. 'The fact that the hard-living group is still at it is an astonishing feat unto itself, but when you realise they're still keeping pace with the younger acts – when it comes to touring and recording – it's even more impressive.'

Lemmy preferred the band's prolific recording pace to

those legendary peers such as AC/DC and Guns N' Roses, who regularly take more than five years between new studio LPs. 'That's what rock'n'roll bands are supposed to do, you know?' he told the *Independent*. 'Get their work out and produce as much as they can. We can do it that fast, so we do. I mean, if it takes your stuff years, like Def Leppard, maybe it's like the way they work, you know. There you go. But I wouldn't trust the public to remember me seven years later.' Moreover, the band's ability to crank out album after album of new material reflected a creative synergy between its members that, as Lemmy explained in an interview with www.poprockcandymountain.com, was instinctive. 'We just do what we always do. We've got it down to a fine art now, you know? We know how to do that now.'

Cameron Webb: '*Motörizer* was more about trying to take what we'd built on the first two records and going, you know what, I felt like I controlled them a lot in the beginning, on the second record, I gave them a little more freedom so, by the third album we made together, I was trying to cross between the two. The other thing was, Lemmy's been getting older and has kind of a does-what-he-wants-to-do attitude, so I was more sympathetic on the last record to times when he really wanted to do something and I wouldn't want something. I would try to be a little soft on him and go, "OK, I believe in you for this but you have to help me out on this other thing." So in a sense it was looser and certain things ended up being more rock'n'roll than if you were to jump back to *Inferno*, where it was a lot heavier of a record.

'I also look at it like: you never know when someone's going to do their last record and, with Lemmy, for what he does, he's a little bit older but still a child at heart. So to me, I never want to be that guy who gave him a record he was unhappy with. I would never want that burden on my shoulders because I make records for artists. I don't make them for producers, I don't make them for labels and Lemmy doesn't either. So on *Motörizer* I was definitely allowing them to be themselves in the studio and respect who they are and what they are as a band with the legacy they have.'

The producer's strategy translated into 'a little bit less pre-production on the third record because they brought me songs that were a little bit more done. With those songs, I actually had some issues along the lines of Mikkey wanting, on one song, to do a double bass all the way through that was similar to a couple of songs on the other records and I said, "Maybe you shouldn't do that. Maybe you should do a different kind of beat in the choruses," and [it] ended up being one of those things we fought about till the day we recorded it and, in the end, I said, "I don't want to do it this way but you're Motörhead and if you really believe it and think we can make a better song than 'Overkill' and all those other songs, then let's do it." And we ended up doing it with a double bass all the way through.'

In another departure, Webb opted 'to track the drums at Dave Grohl's Studio 606, which has a really nice Neve console and a really huge drum room. I mean, the drum room was four times the size of NRG and the vibe there was really comfortable. For *Motörizer*'s overhead drum mics, I used U67s on the overheads with 451s on the ride and hat and, again, I used a 57 on the snare.' And then they were done with the studio, as Lemmy explained in an interview with www.poprockcandymountain.com. 'Just the drums were done up there. The rest of it we did in LA'

Cameron Webb: 'For the rest of the album, the prices at Paramount Studios had gone up a lot, so we had to find another studio, and went to Sage and Sound Studios in Hollywood, which had an API console, similar to the one that I mixed *Motörizer* on. We tracked the rest of the album there.'

This time around, Webb found it a much easier process to capture the bass sound, which Lemmy explained was alive and as well as ever, thanks to 'the new amps they're making for me now – they're called The Lemmy Stack. They're Marshalls and are based around Murder One.' From a production standpoint, tracking that well-established sound went more smoothly. 'By the time we made that record,' says Webb, 'Lemmy walked in the door and I had his knobs already turned the way he turned them, and used the same mics, in general – a 57 on those cabs and a Fet 47 for the bigger cabs.' In an interview with the *Columbus Dispatch*, Lemmy added, 'I have seven Rickenbacker basses but I only use one really. It's the new one. Rickenbacker is bringing out the signature Lemmy bass, which I designed, and it's the most *beautiful* thing you've ever seen in your life! It's all carved on the front with oak leaves and stuff, and they're bringing that out soon. I've got the first one and Rickenbacker has finally made some good pickups! It sounds like murder.'

As smoothly as bass tracking went, guitars proved a different story. 'On the third record the guitar-tracking process became a mess again,' confirms Webb, 'because on the first record, when you're producer, everyone's being really careful, everyone's walking on eggshells – the artist and producer. But once you know someone and are friends with someone and have spent a lot of time with them, you can tell people "no" and you can tell people "fuck off" because you have these relationships that have gone on for several years and albums. So during recording for *Motörizer*'s guitar tracks, there [was] a lot of "no" and a lot of "don't like this/don't like that", so it was difficult. The drama was that Phil knew I was going to ask for certain things and he knew he didn't want to do certain things, so that's where we'd had arguments. Generally, with the solos is where it became more difficult because he sometimes would run out of ideas or would have ideas where I wouldn't like this or that or, if I didn't like it, Lemmy didn't like it and back and forth. So Phil was coming in for a couple weeks, doing a couple solos each day, and I was trying to get him in that magic time where he performed and was happy with what he had.'

There were changes on the technical side, recalls the producer. 'On *Motörizer*, for Phil's guitars, we switched to the Bogner amp, which killed the 900s for that record, so that was used, in general, throughout the album. In terms of why I liked the Bogner, it all goes back to what I was saying about the first LP when I was talking about liking that System of a Down tone and records that had that Slayer tone, and what happens is, when you de-tune a little bit, it keeps the tone heavy and tight and punchy and kind of nasty but smooth, a very brutal sort of sound. And when we plugged in, instantly we loved it because the Bogner sound was bigger than the 900, so we stuck with it. The Marshall is great, I love the Marshalls and those 900s I love to death but, for some reason, this was bigger and more present, and it had super gain. Again, I miked it with a 57 and 421 on the cabinet.'

Offering fans insight into Lemmy's 'Captain of the Ship' role in terms of exercising executive override power on the album's songs, Cameron Webb says, 'Lemmy knows his sound and what people like to here, so you have to let him make those songs he already knows work for him because I don't think Lemmy writes for his fans, I think he writes for himself. As far as Lemmy weighing in on other player's parts, Lemmy allows people to do whatever they want to do when it comes to drums or guitar playing but, if he doesn't like something, he's going to say something. The biggest thing between Lemmy and Phil was that Phil likes to solo really fast and he's great at it but Lemmy likes more melodic stuff all the time. Lemmy likes when Phil goes low on the strings, Phil likes to go high on the strings, so the problem I would run into is that Phil would do a super-fast solo super-high and Lemmy would say, "It sounds like a bunch of wasps in a jam jar," which was his way of saying it sounded like a bunch of noise. And Phil would play good solos, awesome solos, it was just Lemmy didn't always like them.

'So I knew whenever Phil was doing that type of solo and Lemmy wasn't there I was going to get that comment later, and we were going to end up having to re-do it. So there became a point where Lemmy was a filter and I was a filter, basically saying, "OK, you know what, Phil? This is great – I think you did a good solo but you know Lemmy's going to tear this one apart." And some days, Phil would be like, 'Cool, let's try something else," and other days he'd say, "No, if he's not here, he's going to have to come in and listen and then talk to me about this," so it was a give-and-take sort of situation. Phil knew but he wanted to be himself, and Lemmy, ultimately, wanted Phil to be himself, so there were times where he would let Phil just do whatever he wanted. Other times he would say, "Dude, we need to change this solo," and we'd have to bring him in to change [it].'

Lemmy, for his own part, explained to *Inked*, 'We did *Motörizer* the same way we always do albums... We just write the songs and when we like 'em we record 'em. Then we do some more.' Addressing the longevity of the band's loud factor – alive and well as ever on *Motörizer* – he told the *Columbus Dispatch*, 'It's supposed to be loud, isn't it? I mean, what's the point of quiet rock'n'roll? You can have ballads and things but you always have to go back to the killer punch at the end. I just always liked it loud. That's why I always liked Little Richard because he was about as loud as it got back then. I mean, you had Elvis with his well-mannered backing group the Jordanaires humming along and then you had Little Richard, and it's like "Oh, there it is. That's the stuff I was looking for!"'

Addressing the themes of the album, Lemmy continued, 'Sex, death and war. And justice. There's no shortage of lyrics there.' In the same interview, the singer also sought to point out that the songs are far more sophisticated than they're often given credit for, reasoning that people 'miss a lot in Motörhead. They think we're dumb. It just doesn't work that way. Everybody thinks everybody in a metal band or a heavy band is stupid but I don't know why. They're some of the best technicians, especially on guitar, in the world. And bass, I hasten to add. And if you watch our drummer do a drum solo, you'll go away scratching your head if you think he's stupid.'

In an interview with *Inked* on his songs, Lemmy singles out 'one of 'em... about Iraq, "When the Eagle Screams". I wrote that because I know the history of war. I've studied it and this is a prime example of money sending boys to their deaths. The interest's winning over the logic. Everybody knew there were no weapons of mass destruction in Iraq because we sold them everything they had. I'll tell you a funny story. You know when the British invaded Iraq with you guys? We didn't have any desert uniforms. We only had the green and the khaki because we sold all the desert uniforms to Iraq three years before. Isn't that great? I just hate all politicians. They're all bastards.' While the band brought more songs completed to the table ahead of recording on their latest album, Lemmy, in the same interview, added that he still feels he writes some of his best material 'in the studio, under the knife. All our stuff is done with our back against the fucking wall. That's when the hard-hitting stuff comes out.'

Indeed, much of Lemmy's lyrical material for the album came once he and Cameron Webb had begun principle vocal tracking, with the producer recalling that 'on the third album, Lemmy didn't have a girlfriend and I don't want to say he got into a writing block but he had this month before we headed into the studio where he was supposed to be writing lyrics and he wrote, I think, one song in that month. So then, when I brought him in the studio, he got sick and had a cold for the next three weeks, so he'd be writing but he couldn't sing anything and that also made him really frustrated because he couldn't go sing. By the time he got better, he started to perk up and was happier and more inspired, and so when he was doing positive things in the vocal booth, I would try to support and reinforce him. So that third record was difficult because he was sick when we were supposed to be singing and it was hard to write. With Lemmy, unlike other bands, where the studio is strictly for performing and not for writing, with Motörhead it's obviously not that way. I'd go down there and be ready to record and he'd say, "Let me go write this song," and I'd say, "What do you mean, write this song?" And he'd say, "I'm going to write this song today," so I'd sit there next to him and he would write whatever song he was writing, and I'd throw the track on so he could hear it while he worked, or sit and wait, read a magazine and let him work through his process of writing what he was going to write. The last two records were a lot more like that than the first record but they all had that element.'

When he wasn't ill, Lemmy explained to the *Columbus Dispatch* that he didn't do much in the way of special vocal maintenance. 'Out it comes, you know. I have sort of a high voice, really. If you're singing along to something like "Killed by Death", it's tough.' To capture Lemmy's vocal performances on *Motörizer*, Cameron Webb 'used a Neumann U67 on him and, on the third record, because we were recording at Sage and Sound, it was a bigger room I had Lemmy sing in and with the mic up higher and above him, you have a lot of room with the sound. So my biggest thing was I was always trying to get him to sing closer to the mic – even on the first two records, he'd push the mic back and say, "That's not the way I do it," because when he first started doing records, studios wouldn't allow you to be that close to the mic. It was a requirement that the vocal mic be so far away from the kick drum because they were really sensitive mics. So by *Motörizer* I kept trying to get Lemmy to sing closer and closer and closer to the mic, and when I listen to that record I can actually hear, in a sense, a little more depth and room sound in those vocals. That's because, sometimes when I wasn't paying attention, Lemmy would push the mic up a little further, back to where he liked to have it, then when I would come in the next morning I'd push it down closer. So it was kind of a little game of back and forth, and Lemmy didn't probably think too much about it because he does what he wants to do and, if I asked him to sing a little closer, he most times just wouldn't do it. So I had to adapt to that, in a sense.' In terms of a favourite vocal, Lemmy told the *Columbus Dispatch* it had to be 'The Thousand Names of God'. 'I think it's the best on the album. It doesn't grab you the first time. You have to listen to it a couple of times.'

Cameron Webb turned his attention to mixing, quipping that, as quickly as the band banged out songs in the writing process, 'mixing is like going to the dentist and the DMV [Department of Motor Vehicles] at the same time with those guys. It is a friggin' nightmare. I think the first record counts as the best that I did. Other people say they think the second record sounds better – they're different to me. It's a different work ethic, an older-school work ethic, where we'd record for six hours and talk for six hours, and Lemmy would tell these great stories.

'On *Motörizer* mixing was a fucking train wreck because they were on tour and all out of town, so they had to leave town before I started mixing and I would send them the mix on the road, and get these notes back from Phil and Mikkey saying, "It's done, it's perfect, print it." But then I'd get contrasting notes from Lemmy saying, "The bass is too quiet, turn that fucking thing up." Then I'd turn it up and send it back, and the other two guys would say, "It's crap now, give us the old one." Because they'd never mixed a record over the internet, sending mixes back and forth, what would happen was a little trust was lost in that process.

'When you're mixing with someone present in the room, you can basically push a fader up a little bit and find that magic sweet spot, and make them sit there and watch you do it and, if you go too far, they can say so and you can pull back to that magic spot. But when they're not sitting there next to you, watching you do it, they don't think you're actually doing that, they think you're lying to them so you can move on to the next song – not that they don't trust me but, in general, it's human nature to believe I'm not doing that because I can't show them. So there would be some miscommunication at times, where Lemmy would think it was too extreme, get mad and say, "What the fuck are you doing? Can you turn the bass up to a decent level, not this distorting-like-crazy level? Come on, Cameron, get your shit together." So it was a really, really difficult record to mix. I think, at the end, Lemmy was not as happy with me on *Motörizer* because he didn't get exactly what he wanted on that record. The biggest bum-out I got was that I think the bass is a lot louder than it was on all the other records and even read one review from Germany where the critic said, "This record is awesome but, goddammit, why didn't they turn those guitars up? All I can hear is the bass." And I was like, I agree a hundred per cent but it was their record, so I had to compromise more than I wanted to on that record and think it sounds different than the other two, for sure.'

Released on 26 August 2008, *Motörizer*, the band's 19th

studio LP, marked their most successful chart opening in years, with a US No. 82 debut. Even more impressive were the waves of critical raves, beginning with *Hustler* magazine's declaration that *Motörizer* was 'a pummellingly brilliant new CD. Lemmy has never sounded so angry and powerful,' while *Classic Rock* characterised the album as a blueprint of sorts on how to make the perfect metal album, advising all to 'listen and learn'. Concurring, the *Independent*'s music magazine concluded that 'there's a spectacular simplicity to Motörhead's method here', while *Billboard* seemed most impressed by the fact that 'Lemmy Kilmister (who turned 62 in 2007) shows no signs of slowing down on 2008's *Motörizer*, which Cameron Webb produced at Dave Grohl's 606 Studios in Los Angeles. Despite the fact that Webb has worked with a lot of alt.rock and alt.metal artists (including Limp Bizkit, Orgy, Godsmack, Buckcherry, Lit, Ben Folds and Monster Magnet) and produced this 39-minute CD in a studio that is owned by a member of the Foo Fighters and ex-member of Nirvana, *Motörizer* makes no effort to be alternative sounding. Instead, the classic Motörhead sound prevails and forceful, in-your-face tracks... sound like they could have been recorded 25 years earlier... Kilmister sounds inspired and focused throughout the album and at 62 he has yet to overstay his welcome. *Motörizer*... is definitely respectable – and it is good to see this seminal thrash/speed trio still plugging away after so many years in metal's trenches.'

Addressing his stamina after so many years in the business,

Lemmy mused, in an interview with *Rolling Stone*/the *Columbus Dispatch*, that 'my natural fuck-you-ness couldn't allow me to break up the band... We haven't really slowed down too much, have we? But there are different things on different records but always within the genre. We probably should have our own category now – "Motörhead".' In another interview, with *Inked*, Lemmy offered his own assessment of the band's latest studio LP. 'A good album because, I mean, you wouldn't hear it if it wasn't. The only thing that matters is that we like it because we aren't doing them for you, we're doing them for us.'

Cameron Webb: 'One thing Lemmy said to me after we made the 2008 album was, "Two of the best experiences I've ever had in the studio were with you and with Vic Maile on the *Ace of Spades* album," and I asked, "Why?" and he said, "Well, because you let me do my ideas. You don't tell me what to do. You say, "All right, Lemmy, what do you want to do?"

'And I'll sit there and let Lemmy write a song for six hours while I'm waiting for him but, if I don't like something or if I think he can do something better, I'll ask him. And some producers are able to say "try this" or "try that" and he's not that kind of guy because he writes it all. So you have to give him examples of why it could be better if you really feel it could be and then he may go back and rewrite a lyric. I've learned a lot from them when it comes to songwriting and, as their producer, as much as it was about me trying to get them to do things, it was equally about learning from them

244

about what's good or bad and "how can I use this on other records in the future?" Because with what magic Lemmy and Motörhead have, you don't change Motörhead. Motörhead is different than a lot of bands and the cool thing about that is they've always had integrity and done what they wanted to do for all these years. Some people can be successful at that and other's can't, and Motörhead has been, so you really have to trust in the success they've already had and [that] maybe they know something you don't know.'

Reflecting back on his three-LP collaboration with the band, Webb shared that 'for me, personally, I think I actually pulled off miracles with all three of those records, to achieve certain things that I achieved – tightness, bigger, fuller tones, better songwriting and pushing Lemmy to new levels where there were some days where he'd say, "Cameron, I don't want to fucking do this with you today, let's just fucking go home. Don't push me anymore, I'm done, I'm tired of this shit." And I think I'm really proud because I did push those guys and I personally feel like we made some really good records. They have worked with a lot of great producers and I think a lot of those producers pulled some amazing records out back then but, from where I started working with the band, when I compare our records to the couple they'd made before we started… I feel like someone didn't push them as hard and gave them too much freedom.

'I don't look at making a Motörhead record like I do making other records. It's definitely this special thing to me because, in a sense, I think Motörhead was huge when they started, I think they were big for a while, then dove down a little bit and I got into this to pick them up again. I think with those three records I was trying my best to make it current and modern but also keep the band happy. So the legacy weighs pretty heavy but you also have to realise too that you can't be scared of that legacy – you have to embrace it and say, "You know what? Maybe people let you slide on a couple records and I don't want to be that guy who lets you slide." I want fans to say, "That record Cameron Webb did, that's my favourite Motörhead record." I mean, obviously *Ace of Spades* is the album everyone considers to be the pinnacle but I consider the records we made – seventeen, eighteen and nineteet – to be just as strong, and I want people to hear those records and say, "I want that guy to do my record because look what he did with Motörhead!"'

Conclusion

2010 and beyond...

Any study of Motörhead's unsurpassed legacy must conclude, as *Billboard* has, that 'even if Motörhead had broken up around 1983 or 1984, they still would have gone down in history as one of the most influential metal outfits of all time. Motörhead, after all, was the first metal band to seriously incorporate punk; they wrote the book on thrash metal and speed metal in the late 1970s and early 1980s, paving the way for Slayer, Metallica, Venom, Megadeth, Testament, Anthrax, Death, Exodus and countless others. But Motörhead, of course, didn't break up in 1983 or 1984 and they were still cranking out quality albums in the late 2000s.'

The central root of that longevity lies with founder/bassist/vocalist Lemmy Kilmister, who Nirvana drummer and Foo Fighters front man Dave Grohl recently hailed as 'the king of rock'n'roll' and *Spin* magazine celebrated as 'a true legend… worshipped by both punks and metalheads.' Underscoring the latter, Metallica drummer Lars Ulrich, in an interview for the *Ace of Spades'* Classic Albums special, said, 'These guys were cool. At the time there was a big division between the punks and the metalheads but Motörhead broke down all those barriers.'

In response to frequent suggestions that he originated speed/thrash metal, Lemmy routinely disagrees, pointing out that 'Deep Purple was doing things like "Speed King" before we ever came along; they were pioneers of that. There were a lot of bands around that were playing very fast stuff. I think our music is a lot more like pop than metal, if you think about it musically.' Regardless of how the living legend prefers to have his legacy characterised stylistically, virtually everyone – as *Hustler*, for one, recently highlighted – considers his band to be 'one of the most respected and longest-running heavy metal bands in the history of the genre'. *Inked* similarly marvelled at the band's survival. 'Forty years of hard liquor and harder drugs, wild women and life on the road haven't killed Motörhead's Lemmy Kilmister.'

Most feel at this point that the indestructibility of both Lemmy and his band is based, in large part, on what has inarguably become one of rock's most loyal and envied fan followings, summed up in producer Peter Solley's recollection. 'I would walk down the street with Lemmy in

LA while we were making the record we did together and every person that walked or drove by would say, "Hey, Lemmy." He just had instant recognition. And always good vibes. "Hey, Lemmy, what's up, baby?" It was amazing, I was stunned, everyone loved him! He's something special in the world of rock'n'roll. Working with Motörhead is almost the most impressive thing to people on my resume, especially young people. People aren't impressed with Peter Frampton but they love Motörhead.

'I've always said there are "weekend warriors" – some of these bands who *kind of* rock'n'roll – but Lemmy really is everything he appears to be and that's most unusual. When you work with these people, there's always somewhat of a facade but Lemmy really is Lemmy. There's nothing fake about him at all: he's a hard-drinking, hard-drugging, tough son of a bitch! And that's who he is, that's amazing, astonishing. I rank Motörhead right up there and you have to hand it to Lemmy for lasting this long.'

Offering peer perspective, Lars Ulrich told the Classic Albums special that 'it's an attitude, it's a statement, it's a way of life. If you put Motörhead on the back of your jacket or your T-shirt, it says something about who you are and what your beliefs are and what your kind of view on life is. That's an attitude, it's much more than just a relationship between a band and its fans.' That fan base proved itself as alive and well as ever with the www.mtv.com assessment in 2008 that it had 'been a huge year for the Grammy award-winning band, debuting in the

Billboard Top 100 charts and engaging fans with two back-to-back, high-profile US tours.'

Lemmy himself quipped, in his band's most famous anthem, 'Ace of Spades', that 'I don't want to live for ever' but few believe he's anywhere near concluding his career. It's one which renowned producer Tony Platt has suggested places the band 'above Metallica any day. In terms of relevance, in terms of a band that you can say "that band came along and changed things". AC/DC came along and changed things, the Stones did, Led Zeppelin did. There are bands who came along and made a significant difference and then other bands who, in a way, came along and rode on the coat tails of those who made a significant difference. So Motörhead was one of those bands who came along and made a significant difference, I think that's a defensible statement.'

While Lemmy will acknowledge that 'it's nice to be complimented' alongside modern metal icons like Metallica, he ultimately feels that the comparisons aren't important to his own band's survival. 'We're always going to be the only ones doing what we're doing,' he declares. Looking toward 2010 and beyond, his advice for his loyal listeners – old and new – whether in bands or just as fans is, as always, to 'just ignore the trends and do your own thing, straight down the middle. We didn't care about styles going on around us. We knew what we were doing. Trying to fit into the trends will kill you.'

Looking back on his amazingly prolific catalogue of

groundbreaking and genre-shaping albums/hits, Lemmy, in interview with the band's biggest online fansite, www.Motörhead.ru, included among his favourite tracks 'Ace Of Spades'. 'Obviously, because it's clothed my back for the last twenty years. And "Bomber" and "Love Me Forever". "1916", "Don't Lie to Me". Three more? "Overnight Sensation", definitely "Sacrifice", "Over Your Shoulder", and probably "Love Me Like a Reptile" and "Another Perfect Day". That's enough to be proud of.'

Author biography

Nashville-based music biographer Jake Brown has published 21 books, including *Rick Rubin: in the Studio*; *Prince: in the Studio*; *Heart: in the Studio*; *Dr Dre: In the Studio*; *Suge Knight: The Rise, Fall and Rise of Death Row Records*; *50 Cent: No Holds Barred*; *Biggie Smalls: Ready to Die*; *Tupac: In the Studio* (authorised by the estate); as well as titles on Kanye West, R Kelly, Jay Z, the Black Eyed Peas and non-hip hop titles including *Red Hot Chili Peppers: In the Studio*, *Mötley Crüe: In the Studio* and the *Behind the Boards* rock producers anthology series. Brown was also a featured author in Rick James' recently published autobiography, *Memoirs of Rick James: Confessions of a Super Freak* and, in February 2008, appeared as the official biographer of record on Fuse TV's *Live Through This: Nikki*

Sixx TV special, and has received additional coverage and press in national publications including *USA Today*, www.mtv.com, *Vibe* and *Publishers Weekly*, among others. Brown is also owner of the hard-rock label Versailles Records, distributed nationally by Big Daddy Music/MVD Distribution and celebrating ten years in business.